In praise of *Larger than Life*

As Singapore celebrates 50 years of independence, we also celebrate Singaporeans who have left their comfortable homes and ventured into unchartered territories that most of us will not even think of visiting. Their unconditional love shines through like sunlight on a cold, winter day and deserves our respect, admiration and support.

In *Larger than Life: Celebrating the Human Spirit*, we catch a rare glimpse of behind the scenes and first-hand accounts of these stories as told by Belinda herself. I hope you will enjoy this book. Thank you, Belinda, and the production team for bringing all these heart-warming stories to us.

— *Lucas Chow*
Chairman, Health Promotion Board

Belinda shares heart-warming stories of remarkable people who have made the leap of faith to answer their life's calling. It is inspiring to read how they sacrificed creature comforts and material wealth, yet gained a richness beyond what the 5Cs can reap. And that's simply by making a positive impact on another person's life.

— *Georgina Chang*
Head, The Celebrity Agency

Sometimes we take things for granted, and many times, especially in developing countries, we think we are the ones who are being giving. In reality, it is other people whose touching stories enlighten and redefine us. Through the eyes of Belinda, you realise that the most valuable things in life aren't things and we can all make a difference for a better, loving world. This book will expand your capacity to love, to dream, to endure and to find peace in all circumstances. If you don't receive a miracle, you can still be a miracle for someone else.

— *Ignatius Ho*
Vice-President, Life Without Limbs, Greater China

Larger Than Life will give anyone a wake-up call and a different perspective on the really important things in life, especially for those who are too involved in the rat race. Priorities will be explored and nagging questions will be raised about modern-day society and how far we have come, or have we? Singapore's most beloved travel host, Belinda Lee, is not afraid to get her hands dirty and dives headfirst into unimaginable places. The result is a heartfelt read from start to finish. Bravo!

— *Leon Jay Williams*
Regional Artiste

Belinda has always been very compassionate and she has finally found a bridge that connects her true personality to her work and it connects with her audience. It's one thing to see her visit these amazing countries and share the different human emotions from the strength to the joy on television, but to have it in print is just another beautiful extension. Books are food for the soul and in this particular one Belinda speaks for the people and places she's seen and they are able to tell their stories through her.

— *Utt Panichkul*
Regional Artiste/Entrepreneur

For over a decade, the Belinda I know has consistently demonstrated a profound love, compassion and selflessness for those dear to her and even strangers in remote corners of the world. She is always the first to extend a helping hand to those in need and the last to leave in one's personal crisis. Ever since she was little, Belinda has gone through painful experiences that have shaped the woman she is today – a global humanitarian and a community champion whose life mission is to fulfill greater causes than her own. To me, *Larger Than Life* lays bare the core tenets of her soul and is a true reflection of the strength, resilience, and enormous capacity present in one remarkable person. Only one who has experienced life at the darkest depths can turn her mourning into dancing, find the strength to carry others on tenacious shoulders, and bear their weight on calloused but truly beautiful soles.

— *Anne Ng*
Corporate Communications Manager, Lagardère Sports

Belinda and I have traveled the world together sharing deeply profound thoughts and experiences but none have transformed her quite like the ones in this book. I was delightfully surprised to discover that the best part of her travels were intangible. These reflections are for anyone who has ever wanted to develop a deeper compassion for humanity and discover parts of themselves in the big, wide world.

— *Donita Rose*
Regional Artiste

Larger than Life shows that although life can begin with suffering, it should not end so. The overcoming of suffering can be the light and hope of many as there is no better way to thank God than to have compassion and to lend a hand to someone in the dark. This unselfish effort can be the beginning of a fuller life for ourselves.

— *Shirley Tan*
Chief Executive Officer, Rajawali Property Group

LARGER
than life

LARGER
than life

celebrating the human spirit

BELINDA LEE
with JULEEN SHAW

Marshall Cavendish Editions

© 2016 Belinda Lee and Marshall Cavendish International (Asia) Private Limited

Published by Marshall Cavendish Editions
An imprint of Marshall Cavendish International
1 New Industrial Road, Singapore 536196

All rights reserved

No part of this publication may be reproduced, stored in a retrieval system or transmitted, in any form or by any means, electronic, mechanical, photocopying, recording or otherwise, without the prior permission of the copyright owner. Request for permission should be addressed to the Publisher, Marshall Cavendish International (Asia) Private Limited, 1 New Industrial Road, Singapore 536196. Tel: (65) 6213 9300. E-mail: genrefsales@sg.marshallcavendish.com. Website: www.marshallcavendish.com/genref

The publisher makes no representation or warranties with respect to the contents of this book, and specifically disclaims any implied warranties or merchantability or fitness for any particular purpose, and shall in no events be liable for any loss of profit or any other commercial damage, including but not limited to special, incidental, consequential, or other damages.

Other Marshall Cavendish Offices:
Marshall Cavendish Corporation. 99 White Plains Road, Tarrytown NY 10591-9001, USA • Marshall Cavendish International (Thailand) Co Ltd. 253 Asoke, 12th Flr, Sukhumvit 21 Road, Klongtoey Nua, Wattana, Bangkok 10110, Thailand • Marshall Cavendish (Malaysia) Sdn Bhd, Times Subang, Lot 46, Subang Hi-Tech Industrial Park, Batu Tiga, 40000 Shah Alam, Selangor Darul Ehsan, Malaysia

Marshall Cavendish is a trademark of Times Publishing Limited.

National Library Board, Singapore Cataloguing-in-Publication Data
Names: Lee, Belinda | Shaw, Juleen.
Title: Larger than life : celebrating the human spirit / Belinda Lee with Juleen Shaw.
Description: Singapore : Marshall Cavendish Editions, 2016.
Identifiers: OCN 919859637 | ISBN 978-981-4561-18-1 (paperback)
Subjects: LCSH: Voluntarism. | Volunteer workers in social service.
Classification: LCC HN49.V64 | DDC 361.37 — dc23

Printed in Singapore by Colourscan Print Co Pte Ltd

dedication

To God.
And to you, dear reader, who are searching for greater meaning in life.
You are made for greatness.

contents

Foreword by Elim Chew 11
Introduction 13

INDIA
Ravi: Papa of discarded children 16

CHINA
Fang Fang: Mountain medic 38

PHILIPPINES
Rizalito: Living among the dead 60

KENYA
Nicholas: From Katong to Kenya 78

UGANDA
Lesster: The little honey man 104

SHANGRI-LA
Joe & Carol: Making dreams from dust 126

MONGOLIA
David: Feeding the hungry 152

SCOTLAND
Ramesh: More than whole (I) 174

CAMBODIA
Landmine victims: More than whole (II) 190

VIETNAM
Michael: Café counsellor 210

You Can Help Too 230
Acknowledgements 233
About the Authors 236

foreword

by Elim Chew

People have always needed to hear stories — good stories that uplift us especially in busy times when stress can be overwhelming, and inspiring stories that encourage us to keep going even when the going gets tough.

For that reason, Belinda's stories are a welcome source of nourishment for our soul.

The Singaporeans whom Belinda introduces us to in *Larger than Life* are trailblazers, living in unique environments and pursuing unusual passions. They are inspiring individuals in their selflessness, their bold perspectives and their courage in taking the road less travelled.

No matter what their stories, they cause us to reflect on our own lives, touch our hearts and add positivity to our vision.

Belinda's strength is her soft and warm heart, which makes her the right person to share the reflections and values that echo in every tale.

I hope you will be inspired by this book and, better still, go on to inspire others.

After watching the TV series *Find Me a Singaporean*, Belinda connected me to Lesster, the awe-inspiring Little Honey Man and somehow, we just clicked and became great friends.

One thing led to another and suddenly I was on a plane buzzing to Rwanda and saw firsthand his social entrepreneurial work and his expansion plan. Gosh, am I bowled over by the work this man is doing and pleasantly befuddled to find out how small little things like bees can transform people's lives with Lester teaching villagers bee farming skills.

If this short description of The Honey Man piqued your curiosity, then you are sure to devour this book with gusto. Without revealing more so as not to let the insects out of the bag, go on, read this wonderful inspirational story as presented by Belinda.

Elim Chew
Founder, 77th Street

introduction

When I was a little girl, I heard a story that stayed with me for the rest of my life. It went something like this.

One day a boy was walking at a waterfront when he was surprised to come across thousands of starfish washed up on a beach. Knowing that they would die if he did not get them back into the water, he began to pick them up one by one and ease them back into their watery home. A man came along and scoffed, "Why do you bother? It is impossible for you to save all of them!" The boy was undaunted. "I may not be able to save *all* the starfish," he replied as he gently placed another starfish into the water. "But I saved this one!"

The simple story left a very deep impression on me when I was a little girl. While I aspired to be like the boy, I actually felt more like one of the starfish that was desperately but patiently waiting for some kind soul to take notice of me, to gently pick me up and hopefully take me back to a place of warmth and security.

During my school days, I was an introvert. I never took part in any school performances as my classmates told me that I was not talented enough. I suffered from low self-esteem, but it didn't stop me from reaching out to those in need even at a young age. I remember an occasion when I walked home after school one day and saw an elderly man struggling with his bag of groceries. I went over to help him and offered to walk him home. I knew that I would get home late and be scolded by my mum. Yet, I followed my heart and did what I felt was right. The elderly man was so touched that he offered me a drink after I had walked him home. I politely declined and sped off. As I was running home, I felt a warm, tingling sensation. For the first time in my life, I felt a sense of joy and fulfillment. I felt useful. It was a good feeling that was new to me. I was 45 minutes late and, as expected, I was questioned for my lateness. I wanted to lie but didn't know how. Bursting into tears, I told my mum the truth. To my surprise, instead of reprimanding me, she just advised me to be careful when helping strangers.

At the age of 17 after I completed my 'O' Levels, I entered the workforce and did all kinds of odd jobs. In 1998 I plucked up the courage to join the MTV VJ Hunt. The competition was stiff and I was up against very good looking, eloquent and talented people. I felt that I was none of the above. My only saving grace was how big an MTV fan I was. Incredibly, I won the contest and became Singapore's first MTV VJ at the age of 21. I had no idea how I won. Later, the executive producers from MTV told me that I was chosen because of my bubbly personality and infectious laughter which was deemed genuine and refreshing in this superficial industry. "You are a breath of fresh air," the producer said.

After my four-year stint with MTV, I was invited to join Mediacorp, a local TV station. I was given the opportunity to host and act. It was exciting and new, but for some reason I felt that there was something I still had to fulfill in my life which I wasn't doing. This made me sad and a little empty and I considered giving up.

But in 2006, I received a call from my manager that would change my life. It was an offer to host a new travelogue: *Find Me A Singaporean*. This new programme turned my life around. For the first time, audiences saw a side of me that was fun, emotional, inquisitive and vulnerable — the real me. It changed my destiny as an artiste and, more importantly, as a person.

This show took me to far-flung places around the world to look for Singaporeans based overseas. Some gave up a comfortable life in Singapore to pursue their dreams or undertake humanitarian work overseas. They left a very deep impression on my heart. They were ordinary people living extraordinary lives. They exposed me to a world that was filled with love, hope, compassion, meaning and purpose. They opened up my mind to look at life from a different perspective. They didn't need much to be happy. Their objective in life was to help people, especially those in need. Their world was simple, purposeful and unhampered by materialism.

I realised that it is a wonderful feeling to be the real me on television. I started to find meaning in what I did, as every episode that was shown left an impression on the viewers. I received hundreds of e-mails from viewers who poured their hearts out and told me how moved they were after watching the show. It made many of them ponder and reflect on their own lives. It motivated them to be better people and to help those in need.

A deep sense of joy, freedom and purpose was rekindled in me as I interviewed these profiles. My life was enriched, empowered and restored — the same feelings that I experienced when I was a little girl helping that old man. Because of the transformation that I experienced, I thought it would be selfish of me to keep all these amazing stories in my heart and not share them with the world. The stories transformed me and I believed that they will touch others too.

My mentor, Elim Chew, strongly encouraged me to write a book. I wanted to but I had my worries. I didn't know how and where to begin. But Elim told me, "Bel, you are larger than life. Your life is not just about you. It is about other people. Go out there and share their stories. You never know who you will touch."

Life is indeed not just about I, me and myself. We don't need to be a Bill Gates or Mother Teresa to save the whole world. All we need is a willing heart that is never too busy to stop for someone who desperately needs a bear hug or a listening ear. So here I present to you *Larger Than Life: Celebrating the Human Spirit!* It is certainly a dream come true and I sincerely hope that these heartwarming stories will bless you and uplift you, especially if what you are searching for is a purposeful life.

Belinda Lee

Hundreds of Indian street children — rescued, housed and fed by Singaporean Ravi Rai — enjoy a newfound family of "brothers and sisters" in Ravi's five orphanages. Shadowing and interviewing Ravi, the first profile in the *Find Me a Singaporean* series, was equal parts exhausting and exhilarating!

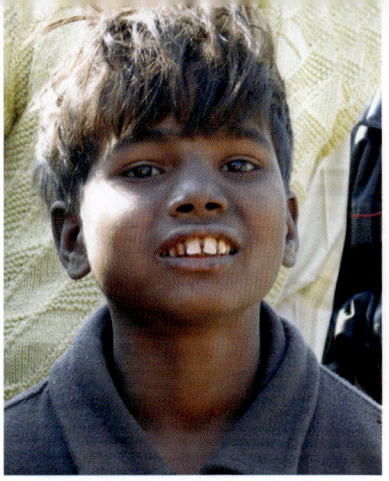

india

RAVI: PAPA OF DISCARDED CHILDREN

The night was just beginning to cast an indigo glow over the dusty New Delhi street as I dragged a brand new suitcase behind me, wincing as it became less and less pristine each time it waded through a grey puddle or ambled over a suspicious patch of mud.

It was a chilly November evening in 2006 and my camera crew and I had just stepped off a flight from Singapore en route to Lucknow in Uttar Pradesh. We were on a mission to find the Singaporean who would kick off the very first episode of the very first season of *Find Me A Singaporean*. What a thrill!

But anticipation quickly wilted into dismay when we discovered that we had missed the last train to Lucknow because of a massive traffic jam. No choice, we had to look for a decent place to spend the night.

Harried by the change of plans and the chaos of rickshaws, scooters, overhead wires, billboards, banners, street shops and milling people, we ducked into the first hotel we saw. Discrimination be damned.

It is estimated that there are 18 million street childen in India, with 60,000 waifs abandoned every year.

Big mistake. When I trudged to my room, I discovered that the door had no lock, just a latch. The walls, originally a baby blue, had decayed to a vomit yellow. The mattress was hollow in the middle and the bedsheet decorated with hair. The shower? It was a hose with cold water.

Jialat, I thought. I'm in trouble!

And that was the start of my challenging journey as a travelogue host. "What on earth did you get yourself into, Bel?" I berated myself as I lay in the bed that was threatening to collapse. Too late — there was no turning back.

Fresh from the glamorous world of MTV VJ-ing and television acting, I had gamely accepted a new challenge: hosting travelogues.

A sense of adventure stirred within me at the novelty. But like a typical Singaporean, my secret hope was that the adventure would not get *too* uncomfortable.

Over the dozens of journeys I would go on to take, from Africa to the Arctic, from Myanmar to Mongolia, I would tackle phobias as I slept in a cemetery, I would scavenge in a dumpsite and stare down swarms of African killer bees. I would be hospitalised for food poisoning, treated for dengue and survive heartstopping dangers. Talk about uncomfortable!

But the real surprise was that this adventure would not only take me around the world, it would also take me on an inward journey of self-examination and self-discovery. I would be challenged, confronted, inspired, and ultimately transformed by the remarkable people I would meet over the next nine years.

My first interview for *Find Me a Singaporean* opened my eyes to the plight of India's vulnerable street children, many of whom fall into prostitution and drug use.

And Ravi Rai was the very first.

***

The streets of Lucknow were haphazard with ringing bicycles, harried pedestrians and wobbly three-wheeled carts piled high with canvas bags overflowing with cotton and vegetables. Traditionally a cultural and historical centre, Lucknow is the capital of Uttar Pradesh, the most populous state in all of India, and also the poorest.

The city seemed caught between tradition and modernity, with suits as common as *sarees*, and contemporary buildings alongside colonial arches.

I must have stopped to ask directions from at least a dozen cyclists and shopkeepers before a group of children recognised Ravi's name and gesticulated excitedly for me to follow them. How telling that the children were the ones who knew Ravi — after all, these youngsters were the very reason Ravi had left Singapore to make a new life in India.

Helpfully pushing and pulling my suitcase, the chattering children led me through an open gate into a field that was bare except for a small huddle of plastic chairs under the shade of a spreading tree.

Perched on the chairs was a fascinating array of children dressed in a motley mismatch of shirts and sweaters and hats, chatting animatedly with a dashing Indian gentleman in their midst.

That was the first time I came face to face with Ravi, then 43, the Singaporean who to this day I call my hero.

***

"Belinda," Ravi greeted with an amiable smile as he rose from his chair.

"Ravi!" I exclaimed, hugely relieved at finally finding this man we had travelled over 4,000km by plane, train and on foot to meet. "Are these your children?"

"These are all my children," he replied with a laugh.

And indeed they were — dozens upon dozens of children, from toddlers to teens, rescued from streets and railway stations where they had been abandoned and discarded.

At that time, Ravi had already set up three homes — places where the children were provided with food, shelter, education, medical care, a stable routine, and more importantly, a family of brothers, sisters and parental figures.

Today, Ravi's Singapore-registered non-governmental organisation (NGO) CoME, or Children of Mother Earth, runs five homes housing some 200 children in Delhi, Lucknow and Gorakhpur in the central northern region of India.

Three of the homes are located in old, disused buildings donated by the Indian railway authorities in support of Ravi's work with the homeless. A medical camp runs on weekends for those who live and work around the railway station: the children, the beggars and the rickshaw pullers.

It is estimated that 18 million street children throng India, with 60,000 children abandoned every year. Without a social safety net, these vulnerable children have very little hope for a stable future. Some are orphans. Others are runaways who have fled a life of abuse.

The children are happiest when Papa Ravi comes home to them.

BELINDA LEE

Yet others have been sold into child labour or the sex trade by their own desperate parents.

Many fall into prostitution and drug use — whitener mostly, hashish if they could afford it.

Ravi developed a routine of taking to the streets and railway stations where many homeless children lived to befriend them and gain their trust.

When CoME began operations, Ravi had asked the rescued children to come up with a name for the orphanage.

"*Apna Ghar!*" came the unanimous reply. As homeless children who'd never had an address, being able to say they lived in Apna Ghar, Hindi for *Our Home*, gave them a wondrous and welcome sense of belonging at last.

The tale of how Ravi came to become Papa to hundreds of lost children is quite extraordinary.

***

Ravi was nine years old when he first visited his ancestral village of Pharsar in the district of Gorakhpur, India. His father and paternal ancestors had their roots in Gorakhpur. His mother was Singaporean, which was how he came to be born and raised in Owen Road, Singapore, the fourth sibling among three brothers and five sisters.

The family was relatively well off, with Ravi's father running a small transport company.

In the Rai family, there was a curious tradition. Whenever the children turned eight or nine, their father would whisk them away to visit his hometown of Gorakhpur.

Top: Apna Ghar, Hindi for *Our Home*, has given the children a sense of belonging.

Centre & bottom: Homeless families are a common sight. This boy living at the railway station shows me how he sniffs glue to numb himself to a life of danger and despair.

A joyful birthday celebration — every rescued child is given a proper name and birth date.

So when young Ravi was nine, he set foot in India for the first time, little knowing that it would be far from his last.

"We drove through the village in our car, a black Ambassador, to our family home which my father had built with his earnings from Singapore," recalled Ravi. "At that time, early 1970s, few people in the village could afford a car. There were only two or three Ambassadors in the entire region! So as we drove to our home, curious village children came running alongside the car, trying to touch it.

"I asked my father, '*Babuji,* who are these children?'

"They are poor people from a low caste."

"What is caste?" Ravi countered. Growing up in Singapore, he had never come across the concept.

"My father told me that the village was segregated into areas for upper caste and lower caste people," said Ravi. "If you were walking along a road, a lower caste person would stand aside for the upper caste person to pass. This is the case even now in the rural parts of India. A social system that has been passed down for thousands of years takes time to change.

"When we arrived at our home, the children stopped at the gate, staring at us. The moment my father called out to them, they ran away. It was clear that they were scared of us, thinking, 'Why are these upper caste people calling us? We must have made a mistake and they are going to beat us!'

"I heard our driver, who was from the village, say to my father, 'Don't have anything to do with them! They are dirty people, they will steal your things!' That was how the villagers thought. But my father stayed silent. "Later on he told me quietly, 'They are not bad people. They steal because they don't have enough to eat. They are poor because they don't have land. They beat their wives because they are not educated.'

"*Babuji* was an open, kind hearted man. In Singapore, he would help new immigrants from India to find jobs. And even when they had secured jobs, he would push $50 into their hands to tide them over until they received their first month's salary. He would call it a loan, but he never accepted payment. My mother was equally generous. She never worked. Well, she had eight children to raise, that was work! But she was always kind to the new immigrants, giving them food, clothes and even our own family possessions like watches. So I learnt compassion from my parents."

To Ravi's delight, his father encouraged him to go to the village to visit the children the next day.

"The children would not come to me, so I went to them," said Ravi, his deep-set eyes twinkling. "I played with them and saw how they lived. A pair of slippers was not even in their dreams. Even the adults could not afford any footwear. If they had a shirt to wear in winter, it was considered plenty.

"They slept on sacks of husks from harvested rice. During winter, if it was very cold, they would pile the husks up into a little hill and burrow inside to stay warm. Those who were lucky enough to have homes, cooked and slept in a single room. The whole family — grandfather, grandmother, parents, children — lived in one room, and the goat would be sleeping in one corner and suddenly a hen would fly across the room! It was eye-opening for me."

***

The memory of the barefoot children who had become his friends and the abject poverty of the villagers never left Ravi's mind, even when he returned to Singapore.

After graduating from university, Ravi earned a good living as a civil engineer in Singapore, and he worked with only one thought in mind: to save money for India. It was the children who had first made an impact on him, and he decided that the children would be the ones he would dedicate his life to helping.

"The poverty cycle has to be broken through the children," Ravi said resolutely. "When parents are not educated, they don't have enough money to educate their children who can't get stable jobs when they grow up, and the cycle continues. So if you want to break the poverty cycle, you educate the children, then the life of this generation will improve and then the next generation, and the next generation."

In 1998, Ravi withdrew his life savings of $300,000 and moved into his ancestral home in Gorakhpur, building a second storey and throwing open its doors as an orphanage.

The first child to arrive was an abandoned one-day-old baby. Next came two five- and six-year-old orphans, a brother and sister, whose father had died in the city years ago and whose mother had recently died in childbirth.

Week after week, he found street children who needed a home. With the help of his sister and local villagers whom he hired as cooks and caregivers, Ravi saw the numbers in the orphanage quickly grow.

"At first the neighbours thought it was a joke when I said I was opening up my home to homeless children," Ravi said with amusement. "When they realised I was serious, they became horrified and said, 'Oh my God, he is going to make our neighbourhood into a low-caste area!' But after awhile, when they saw my passion for their community, they changed their view and accepted the orphanage."

Left: A homeless boy and his pet goat. Right: In 1998, Ravi withdrew his life's savings and moved into his ancestral home in Gorakhpur, throwing open its doors as an orphanage.

Today that one-day-old baby is a well adjusted 14 year old who is enrolled in public school. The siblings have also grown up — the boy has a job in Bombay and the girl recently sat for her 'A' level exams.

***

Wu tiao jian de ai, unconditional love. Ravi embodied that phrase for me, with his extraordinary commitment and sacrifice.

Some of the children Ravi has rescued over the past 17 years have grown up, married and had children of their own, making Ravi a proud "grandpa" of seven.

"Do you ever get lonely? Don't you want to fall in love?" I asked him curiously.

"Sometimes I am a bit lonely," Ravi confessed. "But when I think of my children and how much love they have given me, I feel that I lack nothing. It seems like I am sacrificing but actually I am the one who is gaining a lot from my children."

To illustrate, he told me the stories of two children who have made an impact on him.

Shanti was just seven years old when her prostitute mother was murdered. Together with her mother, her five-year-old brother and her two-year-old sister, they had lived under some plastic sheeting near the railway station. She had never met her father. Her routine every day was to pick garbage and rags from the streets to sell, or earn money from small chores in the neighbourhood.

As she was returning one day from earning a little money as a sweeper, an acquaintance hurried over to tell her that her mother had been beaten up by gangsters. Panicked, she rushed to her mother, whom she found lying in a pool of blood.

The small girl dragged her mother to the road where she managed to persuade a rickshaw rider to take them to the hospital. In desperation Shanti went from one hospital to another, with her mother bleeding out in the rickshaw and her frightened siblings in her arms. Nobody wanted to treat a homeless woman.

Finally, a government hospital staff consented to bandage her mother up before sending them packing. They limped home and the next morning her mother was still alive, although barely. With a few coins she managed to dig up, she bought a cup of tea and bread for her mother. But before the day was up, her mother had died.

What was she to do? The grim skies had opened up and rain was lashing down. With the help of a neighbour she managed to dig a shallow grave and bury her mother in the storm.

Eventually neighbours referred her to Ravi, who took her and her siblings in without hesitation.

"We complain so much about life's little inconveniences," said Ravi. "But here was a courageous little girl who had faced so much at such a young age. Today she is a 14 year old who can still smile after all that she has gone through. What do we have to complain about?"

Mohan is another child who has made a lasting impression on Ravi.

The five-year-old boy lived in a village where thousands were dying from mosquito-borne Japanese Encephalitis, a brain fever.

He was from an impoverished, single-parent family whom Ravi had befriended. When Ravi heard that the small boy had contracted the disease, he had travelled to Mohan's village to try and get him medical help.

All the private nursing homes were packed to capacity and, in 2003, did not have the medication to treat Mohan. Using his influence and promising to bring his own bed, Ravi managed to get Mohan admitted to a medical facility. There, the doctor had told Ravi that within the next 48 hours Mohan would either pull through or die.

"Up until that point, I did not believe in the act of surrendering," Ravi said quietly. "I was an engineer, used to setting deadlines and making projects happen. But that night I prayed for Mohan and surrendered his fate to God. That was a turning point in my life — I began to believe in the value of surrendering."

Against all odds, Mohan survived and has grown into a fine young man. Last year, he sat for his 'O' level examinations.

***

Sadly, not all of Ravi's children make it.

When I first met Ravi in Lucknow, a little boy who hardly reached up to my waist stepped forward and surprised me with a crushing bear hug.

Ten-year-old Anubhav had dark, coarse, patchy skin. When Ravi had rescued Anubhav from the railway station and taken him to the home, the other children had ostracised him because he looked different and did not speak, instead making peculiar, unintelligible noises. In time, with the help of the adults at the home, Anubhav learnt to communicate using language and to socialise with his peers.

During my time at Apnar Ghar, Anubhav soon became my favourite. He was sweet tempered, generous with his affection, and thoughtful, constantly asking me if I had eaten. I remember he was the first one to hug me when I arrived and the last one to hug me when I left.

Mohan, who as a child was struck by the deadly Japanese Encephalitis, survived against all odds and recently sat for his 'O' level examinations.

A few months after the filming, when I was back in Singapore, I heard to my sorrow that Anubhav had passed away.

Ravi had been in London for a training programme when he heard that Anubhav had taken ill and had been hospitalised. Rushing back to India, Ravi spent Anubhav's last 10 days with him in the hospital, bringing him his favourite *chapatti*. In the end Anubhav died in his Papa's arms. I believe Ravi took a long time to come to terms with gentle Anubhav's death.

***

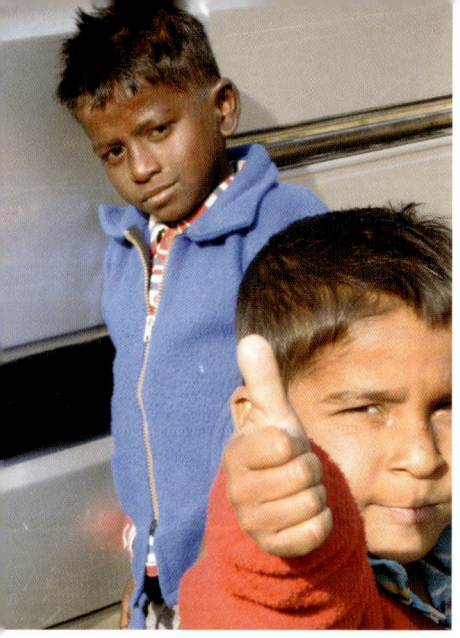

Anubhav (in blue), my favourite child, spent his last days in the arms of Papa Ravi.

There is something very heartwarming about watching a loving father interact with his children in ordinary ways: a joke shared, a rowdy ball game played, a grave exchange when the child misbehaves. That was the way it was with Ravi and his children.

Each morning he would wake up at 5 or 6am together with his school-going children. The teacher he had hired took pains to spend two to three months preparing these illiterate street children to handle the rigours of academia. Up to 98% of his children are enrolled in mainstream schools. Many go on to take their 'O' and 'A' level examinations.

After a breakfast of *chapatti* and milk, there would be a flurry in the kitchen as 40 to 50 school lunches of fried rice or *paratha* were packed for the children to take to school. When it was time for his children to troop off to school, Ravi would send them off with a wave, saying what he said every day, "Happy Earth!"

I watched as four primary-school aged children clambered into an ingenious rickshaw-bus which would take them to school — a cylindrical tin-roofed contraption with benches on either side to fit six small children. It was pulled by a bicycle pedalled by a hardy male staff member.

You would never guess that these children, dressed in smart uniforms with hair neatly combed, were not too long ago wandering barefoot in the streets, their hair matted and their feet stiff with dirt.

When they returned in the afternoon, Papa would be there to greet them and go over their daily school reports, helping them with their weak subjects if necessary. Older children who had problems would steal a few moments to seek Papa out for a listening ear.

When homework was done, Papa would lead the way to the open field armed with cricket bats, marbles, or soccer balls. *Gulli-danda*, a traditional stick and ball game, was a favourite among the children.

Such simple pleasures — and yet so significant to these children who, until life in Ravi's home, had passed their days begging, picking garbage or staying alert in order to escape being waylaid, beaten, or worse.

"When they were living in the streets they went hungry, they went thirsty, they were unable to sleep properly — that is the life of street children," Ravi told me.

Long after they fell asleep in their airy dorms of six to eight beds, Ravi would walk from one room to another, looking on with satisfaction as his children slept peacefully. Occasionally he would find a child tossing and turning, or staring into the darkness, unable to sleep. This troubled him.

"In the beginning I thought that helping the children get a good education was enough. But these children have seen a lot of trauma in their lives," Ravi mused, "things that give them nightmares or make them afraid to close their eyes."

Realising that some of his children needed emotional help, Ravi worked with international counsellors to learn how to help his children come to terms with past hurts.

All of his children's needs — physical, emotional, social, educational and vocational — were considered. He even took it upon himself to find spouses for the children who had grown to marriageable age.

Left: Mealtimes are a noisy and happy affair. Right: After school, some of Ravi's children accompany him to the railway station to persuade street urchins to seek food, shelter and medical aid at the orphanage.

Girls are especially vulnerable on the streets. Once in Ravi's orphanage, they have the opportunity to grow into educated and confident young women.

Sheetal was one such child. She had been a young orphan girl found begging at a temple near the railway station. When the police had brought her to Ravi, she had had a two-year-old brother, Jeetu, in tow. After two days, when she trusted the adults enough to open up, she had revealed that another brother, Chintu, aged five, had run away when the police had "caught" her. She was worried sick about Chintu. The next day, Ravi returned to the temple with Sheetal and after much searching, they found a traumatised Chintu hiding in a pig sty. The three siblings were reunited and 11 years later, an elated Ravi gave Sheetal away as a beautiful bride, playing the role of her father at the wedding ceremony.

***

"The one thing that left a deep impression on me was how happy his children were," my producer Tay Siang Hui commented. "When Ravi stepped into the house, you saw, heard and felt the genuine laughter in his children's hearts. Their laughter rippled through the entire compound and I found myself smiling along with them."

So strong was the impact Ravi had on Siang Hui, in fact, that she made a return visit to India to film a feature documentary on the children living and working around the railway tracks.

It was during that visit that Siang Hui accompanied Ravi on a search.

Ravi had a boy in his home who wished to be reunited with his family. The boy did not remember the name of his village nor the trains he had taken when he had run away. It seemed like an impossible task to locate the boy's village, but Ravi was determined to reunite the boy with his family.

"With every lead he had, Ravi made trips across the country, sometimes commuting on trains for hours," Siang Hui recalled. "I was fortunate enough to be there when he made the final trip to send this boy home to his family.

"The mother's joy at seeing her son again was unforgettable. What broke me was the goodbye between the boy and Ravi, who had been like a father to him. For me to witness Ravi selflessly giving back the son he had rescued, cared for and healed, broke my heart. I saw the pain in his eyes, leaving his child. He did not pretend to be strong, nor did he cry. He commuted home and proceeded to care for all the other children who jumped on him the moment he came back.

Looking at their blithe smiles and merry faces, you would not imagine that these children had not too long ago been destitute and desperate.

> ❝ *In his love, there is often pain. In this pain, Ravi found even more love to give.* ❞

"To say I learnt a lifetime's lesson in humility, love and trust from my stay with Ravi is a huge understatement. In his love, there is often pain. In this pain, Ravi found even more love to give."

***

Ravi took me with him one day on one of his visits to the local railway station. Women in soiled *sarees* slept on the concrete floor as indifferent commuters hurried past. Wild dogs nosed around bodies passed out on the platform. A mound of dirty blankets hid a small child.

That day, Ravi convinced a young boy who looked no older than 11 to return with us to the home. The malnourished, barefoot fellow had no friends, no family, no possessions. He smelt like a pungent blend of garbage, perspiration and excrement.

But Ravi did not seem to notice any of these things. He bent his head close to the boy to listen whenever he spoke and looked at him with a kindly gaze. It was clear that the sorry child he saw before him was not a tattered creature but one who, cleaned up and educated, could become a fine citizen.

Yet this boy, like many, eventually ran back to the railway station after being fed.

Of all Ravi's challenges, the most painful was watching his rescued children return to the streets.

Ravi invested months, even years, to befriend a child and convince him or her to start life anew in one of his homes, only to see the child scamper back to the streets in a matter of days.

"They are used to living in the streets and they feel that they are doing okay, earning enough money from begging to get food, watch a movie or buy glue to sniff," Ravi said without judgement. "By the age of 14 or 15 they often become delinquent or join street gangs. After awhile when they are hungry, they come back again. We have found that on average these children run away from our home three times before they return to stay."

"How do you deal with the disappointment?" I asked.

"It's not easy," he confessed. "You work very hard for someone and at the end of the day they return to the streets. In the beginning the staff and I did get disappointed. But now we are used to it. The children have taught us how to work with no expectations."

Ravi travels by train to one of his five homes every few days, foregoing a comfortable coach for a non-air-conditioned one because "the savings of 500 rupees can buy about 40kg of wheat which can last two or three days in one of the homes".

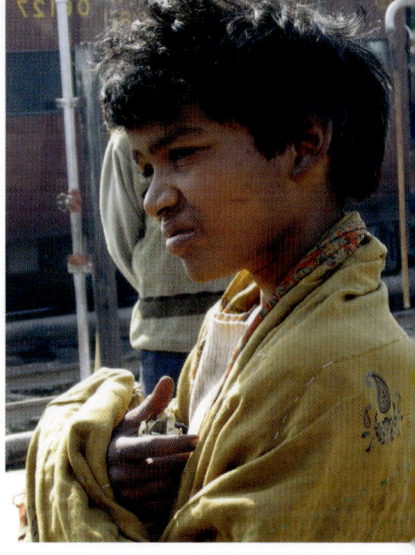

A young boy living at the railway station is persuaded to seek shelter at the orphanage. But like many others, he eventually chooses to return to life on the streets.

Eight months out of a year, when it is not too cold, he drags a simple cot outdoors, sets up a mosquito net and sleeps under the stars.

From the rental proceeds of his three-room HDB flat in Clementi, he keeps CoME afloat, together with support from sponsors.

"When you tell people you are from Singapore, they have respect for you and know that you are not just in the country to make a quick buck," he said. "Whenever I need to meet an official in India, I always mention Singapore and that gets me appointments easily!"

***

Up until then, I had never met anyone who has made such a deep and palpable impact on the lives of so many. Being a handsome and eligible engineer, Ravi had attracted the attention of many a well-to-do family who had approached his parents in the hope of arranging an auspicious marriage.

With bluntness, he had told his parents that he meant to dedicate his life to the street children in India. It was not fair to demand the same dedication of a wife and children, he told them. After barely a moment's hesitation, his parents had given him their blessing. With that, Ravi had given up every comfort he was born with to live among the poorest of the poor.

People often say, "What can one person do?"

I asked Ravi the same question when I saw scores of homeless people begging at railway platforms and barefoot children wandering aimlessly in the streets. There were just so many open mouths and needy palms.

"Yes," he replied serenely, "there *are* so many who need help. But that can't be an excuse not to help them. I do what it is within my capacity to do. And I have found that when you have good intentions with no hidden agenda, help will come."

Ravi gave me a precious glimpse into the heart of a genuine humanitarian and made me realise how incredibly much one ordinary person can do.

***

On our second to last day of filming, our cameraman requested that Ravi and his children wake up at 5am the next day in order for us to make the most of the buttery dawn sunlight.

I said to the children, "Tomorrow morning we are going to wake up at 5 o'clock, and we're going out to the field to film you walking. Is that alright?"

"Ye-e-e-s!" dozens of childish voices rang out.

The next morning, the children popped out of bed with excitement. With their friends, they streamed out of the home into the nearby field of wild mustard flowers. Ravi led the way and his children belted out a cheerful Hindi song as they waded through the sea of yellow flowers waving in the wind.

The chilly dawn air was redolent of flowers. As I breathed in the freshness, I felt like I was breathing in an air of irrepressible hope.

It was not just Ravi who touched me, but his children too. They all had shocking stories. They all had been dealt a tough hand in life. Yet not once did I hear them complain, sulk or wallow in self pity. The simple optimism and genuine eagerness with which they took each day underscored for me the robust power of hope.

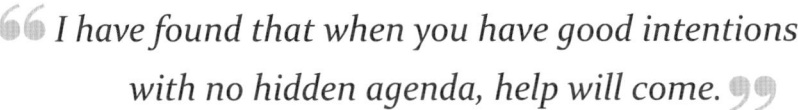

I have found that when you have good intentions with no hidden agenda, help will come.

Nine years later…
I heard from Ravi just weeks after the devastating 7.8 magnitude earthquake hit Nepal on April 25th 2015, taking more than 8,600 lives.

Before the reverberations even settled, Ravi took to the road, travelling some 10 hours by car from India to Nepal with a few of his older teenaged children, braving strong aftershocks on perilous mountain roads in order to render help to the Nepali people.

He had done the same after the Gujarat earthquake in 2002. The thought of children who needed help drove him to reach out with whatever resources he could muster.

Travelling to the Nepalese village of Cougaon, in a mountainous region badly affected by the quake, Ravi put his old engineering skills to use. Together with the Nepali villagers and his children, he built a schoolhouse measuring 7m by 5m from iron pipes and galvanized iron sheets.

That schoolhouse became a shelter for 150 to 200 children between the ages of five and 12. With contributions from well wishers, he bought toys and educational materials for the school from Nepali shopkeepers.

Dawn breaks over a field of mustard flowers as the children congregate for a last group photo. My producer, Siang Hui (right, wearing spectacles), subsequently returned to film Ravi.

It has been almost a decade since I first met Ravi. Evidently, time has not slowed down his drive or blunted his compassion. He continues to role model for his children the imperative of helping those who need help the most.

***

Street children in India possess nothing, not even a name. It is believed that up to 60% of India does not have birth registration. Whenever Ravi succeeds in rescuing a child, the first thing he does is to urge the child to pick a name.

"Some of them take the opportunity to choose names of Bollywood stars like Shah Rukh Khan and Aishwarya Rai," chuckles Ravi. The names are registered with the authorities and each child is presented with an identity card and bank account emblazoned with his or her new name.

Building a schoolhouse for the Nepali children in Cougaon, Nepal, with the help of villagers after the devastating April 2015 earthquake.

"When the children have self esteem, they are less likely to return to a life of begging or prostitution," Ravi said.

No matter the choice of first name, each child of Ravi's also takes on the same surname: Manas, Hindi for *human*. Two years ago, Ravi changed his own surname from Rai — a name well respected in the Indian community — to Manas. It was a gesture that said: We are family.

Like the children, after meeting Ravi I felt as though I had a new identity. One that involved eyes that saw with greater clarity, ears that listened without judgement and feet that hurried a little faster to help someone in pain.

I left India a different person from the one I had been when I'd first arrived.

> ❝ *Their simple optimism and genuine eagerness underscored for me the robust power of hope.* ❞

Top: The hardy Lisu people think nothing of travelling everywhere on foot. Independent young children lugging even younger siblings is a common sight, even on steep mountain trails.
Bottom: Fang Fang visits a villager who has been caged by his family.

china

FANG FANG: MOUNTAIN MEDIC

There was no such thing as roads for the mountain dwellers, only stony dirt trails that turned into muddy slides when it rained. Yet as I carefully picked my way up the tricky mountain path, a wrinkled grandmother sailed past me with a brisk step, her brown face wrinkling as she grinned at my ponderous progress.

Not long after, another villager overtook me easily — this time a young mother carrying her toddler in the front and a live chicken in a basket on her back. Then a young man blithely passed, carrying a solid wooden desk against his back, strapped to his forehead for extra security.

Panting with exertion, I gawked at them as they quick-stepped their way up with the ease of mountain goats. *Should I laugh or should I cry?*

I settled for laughing.

But after an hour of uphill trekking, I stopped laughing when I saw the trail end abruptly in a cliff overlooking a brown river rushing way down below. *Where was the bridge?*

The remote but beautiful Fugong town in the Nujiang Gorge.

"We cross here," said Fang Fang, the slim, young woman my film crew and I had travelled all the way from Singapore to Fugong to film.

"Where?" I was confused. All I could see was a single steel cable that ran from our side of the chasm, floating in mid air a dizzying 10 storeys above the roaring river, and ending in a pile of rocks on the other side.

"See?" Fang Fang pointed along the far end of the cable. As I looked closer, I realised with a start that a tiny figure was whooshing along the cable, a red knapsack hanging precariously off his back as he clung onto a sliding pulley.

"*Aaaaah?!*" I shrieked. "*Zhe yang guo?* You must be kidding, you want us to cross like that?"

The tiny figure rushed towards us and before long was pulling his way along the cable, hand over hand, towards solid ground.

At that moment the young mother who had overtaken me earlier appeared. Looping a sisal rope four or five times around her bum and thighs, she held onto the single pulley and nonchalantly stepped off the cliff, sailing off over the chasm, still carrying her toddler in front and her live chicken behind.

Laughing at my expression of fright, she called out, "*Bu yao pa*, don't worry! My baby has been flying like this since he was one month old!"

That was when I knew that this was going to be a trip like no other.

***

Tan Fang Fang had been just 32 when she travelled alone to Fugong on a crisp winter morning in 2005. She had flown from Singapore to Kunming, then spent 16 hours in a cramped sleeper bus that had driven through the long night up and up into the mountains.

As dawn was breaking, she had finally arrived in Fugong town in the Nujiang Gorge, a place so remote that even many Kunming residents had not heard of it.

Fugong town, plain and concrete-hued, has one of the smallest Han communities in China, with the tribal Lisu people making up 75% of the population.

The most direct way to Fugong is by way of a 16-hour ride on a sleeper bus, with journeys sometimes taking longer if a landslide blocks the road.

We have backpacks, they have baskets! Young and old alike carry all manner of things from live chickens to zinc roofs on their backs.

A hundred years ago, missionaries Isobel Kuhn and James O. Fraser had famously lived among the Lisu. But when the Cultural Revolution fell upon the land, many Christian Lisu had been forced to flee high into the mountains to escape persecution. To this day, Lisu villages are scattered on the slopes of the soaring mountains, accessible only on foot.

A psychotherapist by training, Fang Fang had arrived without a clear idea of what she would do in Fugong. Her churchmate and missionary Dr Tan Lai Yong, who was living in Kunming with his family at the time, had mentioned to her a foster care programme that had been started in Fugong. Her specific role was still a question mark.

Meeting up with the German and Canadian women who had started the foster programme, Fang Fang had politely been told, "I don't think you'll survive here. You should base yourself in Kunming where it's more civilized. At most you can come out occasionally."

Discouraged, Fang Fang had made a call to Kunming and said, "Lai Yong! You asked me to come out here and I quit my job and they don't want me!"

But before Lai Yong and Fang Fang could make any decision, the *100 Year Snow* began to fall.

Despite winter temperatures of 0°C in Fugong, snow typically fell only in the mountains. It had not snowed in town for 100 years! With the unexpected snowfall, roads were closed, communication lines were down and there was no electricity. Fang Fang could not have left even if she had wanted to.

So she had stayed, and as she accompanied the women on their mountain visits to the Lisu, and they saw how her femininity belied a certain toughness, they had told their team leader, "Hey, she can climb. She's okay with the locals. I think she can actually make it here."

So despite her tremulous beginnings in Fugong, Fang Fang became the first and only psychotherapist among the Lisu, pioneering a mental health programme for the mountain dwellers.

***

Several times a week, Fang Fang would catch a *san lun che,* three-wheeled taxi, from her apartment in Fugong town to the foot of the mountains, hike an hour uphill to the zipline, fly across precariously, and trek one to two hours further to different villages on the mountain slopes. There she would visit women and children in the foster care programme as well as mental health patients and their families.

As my crew and I panted our way up the mountains, trailing Fang Fang on one of her regular climbs, we were bewitched by the view. In the west the Gaoligong Mountains stretched up to a height of 4,000m and to the east the Biluo Mountains soared even higher. From our vantage point, the green peaks rose and fell one after another like the jagged back of a jade dragon.

When we reached the zipline and I caught sight of the villagers sailing across the ravine with no safety harness whatsoever, I squeaked, "Just watching that makes my legs go soft" to which Fang Fang calmly replied, "It's okay, you won't need your legs for this."

We shared a hearty laugh and Fang Fang added that she had even seen cows being ziplined across!

"It can't be very comfortable for the cows," she added wryly.

After watching the young mother and her toddler fly across, and then a couple of young boys who zipped across toting a bamboo pole and various other sundries, waving a merry *"zai zian"* to us, I finally plucked up my courage to literally jump off a cliff.

Clinging to an attendant villager for dear life, I put my weight on the rope under my bum and… *off we went!*… zipping across at high speed over the rushing river. A few metres from the end, we ran out of momentum, and the villager pulled us towards the rocks using sheer arm strength. Had the acceleration been too great, he would simply have slowed us down by wrapping a rubber slipper or a bunch of leaves around the cable.

I had made it to the other side in one piece!

Gleefully, I clapped my cameraman on the back — he had gamely flown across with his camera in tow!

Fang Fang mumbled sheepishly, "My mum is so gonna kill me when she watches this on TV. I didn't tell her that this is what I do every week."

On the other side of the zipline, we still had a two-hour climb to our destination. Puffing with exertion and holding onto one end of a bamboo pole while Fang Fang tugged me up the the slope with the other end, I managed to wheeze, "The more I climb, the more respect I have for you and your job. You mean you have to climb like this all the time? So high, so far, with such difficulty, just to see one patient?"

"God made me for hard places," replied Fang Fang with a smile. "In the biography of Eric Liddell (*Chariots of Fire*), he said, 'When I run, I feel the pleasure of God.' That's exactly how I feel when I walk up the mountain. I just love it.

"But really, it is the people who make this worthwhile. The Lisu are very special — loving and kind. Even when they are the poorest of the poor, they have an air of contentment. I hope to be able to give them some measure of comfort."

Arriving at a village, I became Fang Fang's assistant as she engaged a group of eight young women who were fostering orphaned children. The foster care programme helped orphans to remain in their own village and retain their Lisu roots.

With her amiable manner, Fang Fang managed to draw the women out of their shyness to do some roleplay, sometimes to hilarious effect. She talked to them about hygiene and the use of emotional language when caring for a child. Sometimes the orphans were traumatised or had mental challenges, which made fostering more difficult.

Filming among the soaring peaks. The only way up is on foot, even if you have to carry your cow up the mountain.

"Lisu women have led tough lives and are such an isolated people — their cycle of life is confined to their little village. Many women have never even come down the mountain to the town!" said Fang Fang. "They don't speak anything but Lisu. Learning emotional language shows them how to be more tender."

Fang Fang had 65 families in her care whom she and her Lisu mental health team visited on rotation — some were foster families while others had family members with schizophrenia, bipolar disorder or depression.

***

Nine-year-old Ah Na was an orphan who lived with her foster family in a flimsy bamboo house on stilts with rattan-matted walls typical of Lisu homes.

Four years ago she had been orphaned when her parents and older brother had been swallowed up in a landslide. An elective mute, she had not spoken since the accident.

"Hello, *Ah Yi*," Fang Fang greeted Ah Na's aunt and caregiver when we visited. *Ah Yi* smiled widely and beckoned Ah Na forward.

Orphan Ah Na, a traumatised child, stopped speaking after her parents and brother were swallowed up by a landslide.

A slight girl with short, straight hair approached and shook our hand wordlessly. She had the wide eyes and shyness of a doe, ready to bolt at the slightest excuse.

Ah Yi brought us glasses of water, which she set on the rattan floor where we sat. There were no chairs.

"Ah Na was a traumatised child, but she's much better now," Fang Fang told me quietly. "It used to be that if you spoke A BIT LOUDER, like this, she would cry. She was a very, very frightened child. She's much less withdrawn and much more responsive now."

A few other children, from toddler to pre-teen, were gathered in the house in anticipation of Fang Fang's visit. Digging in her bag, Fang Fang produced a handful of balloons and stickers to the delight of the children, including Ah Na. One or two crawled into her lap as she sang to them and let them choose stickers which she gently stuck on their ear lobes as earrings.

By encouraging Ah Na to play and communicate with other children, Fang Fang hoped to reintegrate Ah Na and other orphans into their society so they would not be marginalised.

The happy scene was replayed at the next home we visited, where orphaned Ah Cha was living with her older sister and nephews. Ah Cha was 12 or 13 but was so undernourished that she was not much bigger than her five-year-old nephew.

Her house, like so many Lisu homes, was perched precariously on a mountain slope. It made me nervous to look up at the toddlers waving to us from the open, rail-less verandah of their home set on high stilts. Making our way up to their verandah, I stopped short. The floor was simply made of rows of tree branches with yawning gaps in between, through which the ground was visible far below. *How do I walk on this?*

I clung onto whatever support I could and marveled at how Fang Fang strode across the flimsy floor.

A typical Lisu dwelling of bamboo, rattan and zinc, often precariously perched on a steep mountain slope.

When Fang Fang had first met Ah Cha, who was developmentally slow, she had been a wild-looking girl who had not known how to interact with people.

"We were a big part of Ah Cha's life from the age of nine," said Fang Fang fondly. "Almost every week we would visit her. She knew my name and would look out for me.

"When I first met her, she looked like a boy and she could barely talk. She was feral and her hair had lice. Her sister said she was slow, she was crazy. But once my Lisu teammates and I started visiting her, teaching her how to read and write and speak, she showed a great personality with a sense of fun and adventure. In any society she would have fallen under the helpless and needy

Ah Cha, a loving child who is developmentally slow, was dubbed "crazy" by relatives.

category, and yet she took care of the younger children and was such a giver, sharing the best of the little treats we brought. She was not sweet but she was spunky and had a zest for life, not ever thinking of entitlement or that anyone owed her anything. It's hard not to love someone like that. My local staff love her very much too."

As we played with the children, Ah Cha's sister and brother-in-law were squatting over the hearth, where a wood fire was crackling, radiating as much smoke as heat. Ah Cha's brother-in-law produced a whole chicken and proceeded to chop it up, cooking it in a blackened wok over the fire.

Gathering around the red glow of the flames, we sat on the floor where the family had placed our bowls of rice and chicken. Meat was precious, Fang Fang whispered to me, but the Lisu families were so hospitable that they would slaughter their only chicken to provide us with a meal even if it meant that they had to go without meat for months afterwards.

The third child we visited was a toddler who had been severely scalded on both legs when he had walked into the hearth and stepped in a pot of boiling pig feed. The hearth was the heart of the Lisu home. It was where the family and the family dog gathered to keep warm, to cook their pig feed, and prepare their own meals. To have an open, unprotected fire on the floor where babies and toddlers play must have been a safety hazard. But that was the way of life for the Lisu.

I winced at the sight of the peeling skin on the toddler's legs and the raw, pink flesh underneath. Fang Fang snapped on a sterile glove, applied salve to the wounds and bandaged the legs as the baby wailed with pain. Picking him up, she cooed and bounced him until his tears turned into gurgles of laughter.

In that instant I saw that Fang Fang's role was not just to change a dressing or teach the villagers hygiene. Her very presence brought comfort to them. This had everything to do with her genuine concern. Whenever we arrived at a home, they welcomed her like a sister and a friend, not a social worker.

As we left the grateful mother, Fang Fang confided, "Sometimes I really wish there were professionals who have all the skill and all the knowledge to come out here. It's a challenge for me because I have no medical knowledge. I would love to see the Lisu get the help they need."

***

The next day we were back on the mountain with Fang Fang… ziplining was fast losing its terror! This time we were visiting one of Fang Fang's mental patients and his family.

Ah Chi was special to Fang Fang — he had been her very first patient.

Ah Chi's family lived in a particularly remote village. The higher up the mountain we climbed, the more barren the landscape and the meaner the homes. Eventually we were so far up that we seemed to almost be at eye level with the clouds that wreathed the distant mountains.

A fire is kept burning for warmth in the middle of the house, where all the cooking is done. A toddler, who was severely scalded when he stepped into a pot of boiling pig feed, has his wound dressed by Fang Fang.

At the doorstep of Ah Chi's family home, we stopped abruptly. Fang Fang pointed a little way down the side of the mountain to a ramshackle enclosure that looked like it had been cobbled together with whatever was available on the mountainside — twigs, dried leaves, bamboo and natural rope. It appeared to be a basic shelter for livestock and I was surprised when Fang Fang said, "That is where Ah Chi lives."

I was bewildered. "You mean he doesn't live in the house with his family?"

"No. He has been caged for eight years in a pen after he burnt his family's house down," Fang Fang replied. "He had a reputation. People were afraid of him and thought he was demon possessed. His schizophrenia caused him to hear voices in the middle of the night and he would sometimes sing and talk to himself, scaring everybody around him.

"He is not the only one. There are many around here who have been caged up or chained by their families."

This was not meant to be an act of cruelty, but one based on communal good, she explained.

"The decision the family has to make is not just about the individual. They are also thinking about everybody else living in the village and their well-being, how it would affect the community if their son attacked somebody."

Fang Fang led the way into the enclosure. As my eyes adjusted to the dimness, I saw a rectangular pen made with horizontally placed logs on four sides and over the top, each log the width of a man's leg. There was no door. Wide gaps between the logs allowed the elements in. The thatched roof high above the pen would not have stopped rain or snow from blowing in.

On the dirt floor of the pen sat a young man of 26, huddled silently under a thin, red blanket. We bent over to peer through the gaps and when Ah Chi raised his head, I gave a little gasp.

I had expected a wild looking fellow, not this handsome lad with short, black hair, natural sideburns, a distinctive nose and dark eyebrows over intelligent eyes.

The fact that he looked like he was in the prime of his life broke my heart.

Fang Fang treks for hours to visit her Lisu patients, including those who have been caged by their families. The man within this pen once walked several hundred kilometres when he was suffering from a psychotic break.

The pen was hardly long enough for him to stretch out when he lay down and from the centre he could have reached his hands out and touched either side. Neither was it high enough for him to stand up without crouching, which meant that he had not stood upright for eight years.

"Hello, Ah Chi," said Fang Fang. I bit back my emotion as I reached into the pen to shake his hand. He took my hand and gave a small smile.

Fang Fang's translator, De You Sa or Ah De, handed Ah Chi a bun and he accepted it wordlessly, taking small bites with downcast eyes.

"This is one of his better days," said Fang Fang softly.

Peering into the empty pen with mats for flooring, I asked, "How does he shower?"

"No shower. He urinates in that corner."

"What was he like when you first saw him?"

"Naked. He didn't like to wear clothes. His pen was very dirty. He was screaming at nights, hurling things because he hears voices. The aim right now is just to get him familiar with us, to be friends with him. To show him that there are people other than his mother who care for him and like to talk to him."

Squatting so that she was at eye level with Ah Chi, Fang Fang asked him, "*Ni de yifu hai gou ma?* Are your clothes sufficient?" There was no reply.

To Ah De, she asked, "Is he wearing shoes?"

"No, he's barefoot."

"Does he want shoes?"

Ah De spoke to Ah Chi in Lisu and for the first time I heard Ah Chi's voice as he spoke in low tones into his bun.

Ah De translated, "He said you had told him you were going to bring shoes."

Fang Fang apologised profusely, "*Ah! Dui bu chi*, I'm so sorry, I must have forgotten! Okay, okay, I will get him some shoes as soon as I go down the mountain… *zao gao le…* that's terrible!"

Ah Chi gazed at us then, a smile playing around the corners of his lips, amused at Fang Fang's embarrassment.

"Stick out your foot, let me draw it on this piece of paper," said Ah De to Ah Chi, who mumbled a reply.

Ah Chi in the bare pen he was confined in for eight years. Shaking his hand that day was very special to me as he was not always lucid or approachable.

"Oh, he knows his shoe size, it's 42!"

There was a moment of levity as we all laughed at his cleverness and our clumsiness. Ah Chi smiled too, pleased to have made a joke.

In a moment it was time to go and I shook his hand again as he watched us leave.

Outside, I asked Fang Fang a question that had been playing on my mind.

I was puzzled. "How did they force a fit and strong young man of 18 into that pen?"

"Actually," Fang Fang said, "everyone had told him he was crazy. He believed them. So he sat down and allowed the pen to be built around him."

I had been biting back my tears but at that revelation, I could hold them back no longer. Oblivious to the camera, I broke down and wept.

I cried for Ah Chi, for the dignity in his eyes, for his lost years, for the utter desolation he must have felt when he sat in the dirt as the sound of nails being hammered into the logs reverberated around him. I cried for the fortitude with which he bore his fate, willing himself to live in the cage for as long as it took. I cried for the glimmer of hope he must have nursed, despite everything, to have survived the harsh elements for eight long years.

As a child I, too, had felt a sense of rejection. I was a disheveled child who had only one pair of school shoes and a mended uniform. I had been told time and again that I was good for nothing, that it was better that I was given away, that I was better off not being in this world. So when I heard of

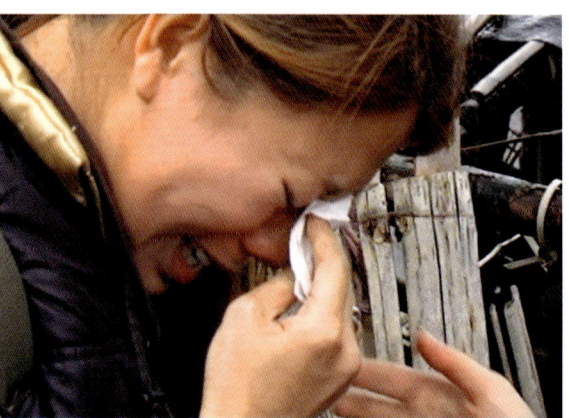

The plight of Ah Chi had me weeping on national television for the first time.

Ah Chi's rejection, the force of his plight hit me intensely.

My producer, my cameraman… none of us was unmoved by Ah Chi's stoicism.

Then dimly, through my tears, with the camera still rolling, I realised that Fang Fang was awkwardly peering into my eyes and whispering something that sounded suspiciously like, "Lashes… your eyelashes."

I had cried so hard that one of my fake eyelashes had dislodged itself and was flapping on my cheek like a lost caterpillar. Too distressed to be much bothered, I said, "*Eh? Oh.*" and yanking it off unceremoniously, tucked it into my pocket, all the while continuing to weep.

My cameraman had to turn off the camera as our tears dissolved into laughter.

Still chuckling, Fang Fang said, "You had taken so much trouble with it, even waking up early this morning to put on your eyelashes. I was worried that it might be your only pair of fake eyelashes and there is still more filming to do!"

That light-hearted moment eased the heaviness in our hearts.

Much later, I asked Fang Fang how she had felt when she had first set eyes on Ah Chi.

"Actually I felt more for his mother," she admitted. "She was a shy, timid, longsuffering woman and she really loved him. But she also had to please her husband, Ah Chi's stepfather. She had married another man who had graciously taken in her son, but there was pressure on her to keep him out of the way.

"For Ah Chi, there were moments when his illness had taken over so much that I could not see much of his personality. But I could see the anguish in his mother's eyes."

Ironically, the mother's helplessness had found an echo in Fang Fang's heart. *How was she, a city girl, to help Ah Chi in these remote, rural surroundings?* There was no medical or therapeutic model she could follow. *What could she do?* In Singapore Ah Chi would have been diagnosed by a chain of professionals, including a medical doctor, a psychiatrist, a social worker... here there was nobody to help him.

She wrote to different organisations who ran rehabilitative communities, but none offered any useful advice. In desperation, she wrote to the author of a series of books meant for missionaries travelling to remote places.

The books had such titles as: *Where There's No Doctor*, *Where There's No Vet*, *Where There's No Dentist* and, lo and behold, one was entitled *Where There's No Psychiatrist*. The author, a British professor of Indian ethnicity, replied Fang Fang's e-mail and encouraged her to visit a leper community in India to see how they ran the commune.

Flying to India, Fang Fang drove many kilometres to find the leper community blooming in the middle of nowhere. It was said that many lepers were hiding their illness because the moment their family knew they had leprosy, they would be buried alive. A building contractor had embarked on a project to build shacks for the lepers who had been forced to flee from their own families. The community had grown to include a hospital and doctors.

At the hospital, Fang Fang met a remarkable doctor who had graduated from Australia but had returned to India to serve the outcasts. To Fang Fang's desperate questions, he replied gravely, "You might have to be the first to start a new mental health model in Fugong."

So she did. She visited her mental health patients as regularly as she could, making sure they were being treated humanely and counselling the families as well. Her overarching goal was to be faithful in small things, to see what she could do for each patient in order to make his or her life more meaningful even if their condition stayed with them for life.

"The Lisu have a name, *qo-ko-la-ma*, *qo-ko-la-pa*, meaning crazy girl or crazy boy. They use this as a dumping ground and anybody they can't explain falls into this category," said Fang Fang. "I helped them to think in new categories, to show them that their child was not cursed, that his condition was not because some great grandfather had done something terrible and visited a curse upon a generation. There was a lot of that kind of thinking. The new category would be: There is such a thing as mental illness. In the same way you can have an accident and be physically hurt, sometimes people encounter emotional incidents that hurt them psychologically.

"To their credit, they never thought of abandoning their loved ones. But they were very poor and if they had a son who was burning their neighbour's field or destroying property, the family had to pay and they just could not afford it. So the only thing they knew to do was to lock him up."

The results of Fang Fang's visits and care were tangible. Families saw their loved ones improving, and the project grew fast. The villagers started calling her *nye-ci-si-ma,* or doctor, which Fang Fang initially objected to, saying, "*Mang-a,* no I'm not!" But the villagers persisted in dubbing her Medicine Woman Fa Fa and eventually she gave up correcting them.

With pressure from Fang Fang and her Lisu mental health team, some caged patients were even released.

"Sometimes the release is quite emotional," Fang Fang said. "Some patients have elderly parents who really love their children. It was a big thing for them to let go of their fears, to dare to believe that their son would be okay, that he would not beat them up when he was released. Family members and villagers are often present at the release, curious to see what happens."

Of Ah Chi, Fang Fang said, "I'd like to see him recovered. I'd like to see him in the fields working with his mum. To start with, I'd like to see him able to walk freely. I think he can go far because he's improved so much even in the short time we've been with him."

It was a few months after our filming and I was back in Singapore when I received word from my producer that Ah Chi had indeed been released. We were overjoyed.

Fang Fang, who was present at the release, told us that it had been a quiet affair as Ah Chi had a small family and his village was very remote. When he was helped out of the pen, he had not displayed any emotion, perhaps because of the effects of his anti-psychotic medication. There had been no tears, no hugging, but his mother had been visibly moved. She had shown her affection in the only way she knew how — by feeding him. Then he had gone into the house. Eventually he even began helping out at home with the household chores.

***

Fang Fang impacted me in a way that no other person had. She and I were close in age. She was well educated and could have led a comfortable life in Singapore. Instead she had travelled to a remote backwater to help people who had no one else to help them.

We often look to our seniors to be our mentors. But Fang Fang was a young woman, a peer, who had not let youth get in the way of her ideals. It made me realise that age plays no part in the impact we can make.

> *It made me realise that age plays no part in the impact we can make.*

Fang Fang showed care for the Lisu people not just professionally, but in the way she made them feel valued. I resolved to do the same for my own personal relationships.

On our last trip down from the Fugong mountains, I had a frightening accident. We had been trekking for so many hours with so little to eat that on the last slope, my legs just gave way. I slid backwards down the trail and if not for the fact that Fang Fang had been behind me, stopping my downward slide, I would have rolled right off the cliff.

That incident shook me and made me realise just how much danger Fang Fang regularly put herself in for the sake of the Lisu families.

Of course she modestly disagreed.

"I'm just so glad that I didn't miss out on the opportunity to come here," she said humbly. "Just by good fortune I managed to find this tiny corner of the world — such a beautiful place — and to be part of this beautiful community. I couldn't wish for anything else."

***

A year after the filming…
I was at a photo shoot in Singapore. Tasked to bring some of my belongings that meant a lot to me, I had specifically chosen to bring along a pair of sneakers that I had bought in Fugong. It was identical to the pair I had bought for Ah Chi before I left — an inexpensive, made-in-China pair with a camouflage design.

I was doing my make-up and was feeling rather buoyed because I was looking forward to sharing about Ah Chi.

Out of the blue, my phone rang. It was my producer.

"Ah Chi has passed away," she said soberly.

I was in shock. "No, no, no. What happened?"

"I don't know," was the reply.

It was very, very difficult for me to contain my tears for the photoshoot.

Much later, I spoke to Fang Fang who told me that she had been conducting training that day when she received the news from her translator Ah De.

"I cried so badly," Fang Fang admitted. "I cried and I cried and I still had to go to the funeral, where I sat with his mother and we cried together. I don't think I ever felt like that again with any other villager. He was my first patient. I had such high hopes when I heard how well he was doing. It felt like he had come out of such a dark place. This was so unexpected."

There was no post mortem. Fang Fang was told that he had turned catatonic one day and, out of ignorance, was put in the house without a drip or any water for a week. His organs would have failed.

Fang Fang said, "When he died, someone asked me, 'Can you bring some meat?'"

It was the custom at Lisu funerals to kill a pig to feed the villagers who helped with the burial. But Ah Chi's family was so poor that they had no pig to slaughter.

"How do you recover from something like this?" I asked her tearfully. If I had such a strong reaction after meeting Ah Chi for just a few minutes, how much more devastating this news would have been to Fang Fang.

She did not reply immediately. After a moment, she said, "The greatest gift I can give to the people I counsel is to have the exchange between us be genuine. Not just charitable relationships but genuine relationships. And that was what I had with Ah Chi.

"There is redemption in relationships," she concluded with conviction.

I have remembered her words to this day.

> *The greatest gift I can give to the people I counsel is to have the exchange between us be genuine.*

Manila North Cemetery, the largest and oldest cemetery in the capital, is a "hidden city" of busy streets, homes, vehicles and throngs of families.

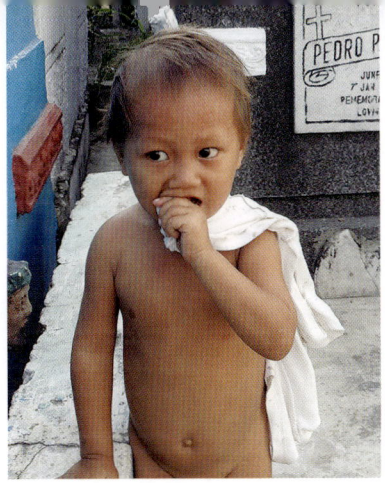

philippines

RIZALITO: LIVING AMONG THE DEAD

All the ghost stories I had ever heard came flooding back to me, making my knees wobble like *agar agar* and my mouth turn dry as a coconut husk.

It was the dead of night. The deep darkness enveloped me as I picked my way around the ghostly silhouettes of crumbling tombstones.

The only sounds were the mournful creaking of cicadas and my shoes crunching on gravel and dry grass. Candles flickered here and there, casting an eerie glow on the names of people long gone. My torchlight threw a shaky circle of light on the ground.

"I am not scared, I am not scared," I repeated… successfully scaring myself witless.

Up ahead a figure sat on a tomb, silently staring up into the black trees looming over him.

"Hello?" I called out, my voice squeaky with fright. "Hello? I am looking for Rizalito?"

He turned and said, "Follow me."

Pushing open an ornate iron gate, he beckoned to me to enter a crypt the size of a small room, musty smelling and bare except for two rectangular tombs and a stone shelf where the feeble light from a few candle stubs wavered.

"I have made special arrangements for you," he said in Tagalog.

"Uh huh," I replied uncertainly, not quite comprehending.

"Bye bye!"

Was that glee I heard in his voice? He turned abruptly and disappeared into the night.

Suddenly it dawned on me what the sleeping arrangements were.

"*Eh... ni...* " I managed to stutter, one arm upraised, before he was gone.

No choice. I unrolled my sleeping bag and placed it beside the tomb. Squeezing my eyes shut, I tried to get some sleep.

After three hours, I still had not slept a wink in this strange crypt with shadows flickering on the hoary walls. With a sigh, I gave up.

***

A sleepless night among the tombstones.

The next morning, bright and early, Rizalito returned for me.

In the morning light, nothing looked as spooky as it had a few hours before. Rizalito Sevilla, a short, slight man with a weathered face, was sporting a cheerful, yellow, soccer t-shirt, shorts, flip flops and a jaunty, purple cap.

My camera crew and I were here at the Manila North Cemetery to film Rizalito for the travelogue *The Places We Live In*.

I trotted beside Rizalito as this spry 52-year old led the way to the home where he lived with his wife Ophelia, his 19-year-old daughter and 10-year-old son.

Rizalito was born in the cemetery and has lived within its walls his entire life.

"Where is your house?" I asked him curiously.

"Street 38," he replied with a smile that had a few teeth missing. This sounded normal enough, except that Street 38 was actually a cemetery thoroughfare.

With a population of about 12 million, metro Manila is one of the most densely populated urban areas in the world. Up to 40% of its residents live below the poverty line.

Left without housing options, these bottom rung dwellers began to populate the largest and oldest cemetery in Manila by the thousands, turning a century-old abode for the dead into a thriving city for the living.

It is believed that there are about 10,000 people living in the sprawling, 54-hectare Manila North Cemetery. Squatters have made this their home for so long that some have been born, lived their entire lives and died within these cemetery walls. Rizalito's mother was one of those people.

Why on earth would people want to live in a place like this? I wondered. *Why are they not afraid?*

That is what I was here to find out by stepping into Rizalito's shoes for a few days.

About 10,000 people, young and old, live in this sprawling "town".

As we walked, I looked about me in astonishment. This was not a quiet cemetery… this was a noisy, bustling town!

A motorbike sounded its horn loudly as it whizzed by, giving me a fright and making me jump out of the way.

I had to watch out for crazy traffic in a cemetery?

Cars and motorbikes hurtled down the streets, housewives fried up lunch on kerosene stoves or sat gossiping in front of their homes, children played with pet mongrels in the street, couples strolled past, vendors sold snacks and soft drinks from makeshift stalls, teenagers danced to music, and men, young and old, went about their jobs.

Residents even made a living in this hidden city. The only clue that this was not a normal town was that instead of buildings, every street was lined with tombs and mausoleums, and every so often a funeral hearse would pass

Life in the bustling cemetery.

by with a sad procession trailing behind. In this busy cemetery, there were 70-80 funerals a day.

Instead of playgrounds, children sat atop stone tombs playing dice or strumming guitars.

They did not mean to be disrespectful. This was their home, not by choice, but by necessity.

***

Ducking between streets, Rizalito and I found ourselves at one of the many funerals taking place. A crowd had formed, including family members of the deceased and residents of the cemetery hoping for work.

"This is how we earn our living," Rizalito said matter-of-factly, as he joined two men who were heaving a coffin into a third-storey tomb.

Space is at a premium in this crowded cemetery and many concrete tombs are stacked up several storeys high. The buried, whose relatives cannot afford to rent a single tomb, share space with other occupants.

Pushing the coffin into the cavity of an open tomb, the men proceeded to seal the mouth with cement. Such work earned each man S$1.50.

Just before the tomb was closed up, Rizalito removed a yellow canvas bag.

"Can you hold this?" he said as he handed me the bag.

"Sure," I said, not thinking too much about it. Was there cement inside? Perhaps some old belongings?

"What is it?" I asked.

"Bones," came the reply. "Human bones."

Evidently the family had defaulted on rent for the tomb and the skeleton had to be evicted.

Left: Many hands place a coffin in its final resting place for the sum of a few pesos.
Right: Rizalito works at sealing a tomb with cement, a job that earns him about S$1.50.

I gulped. The bag felt heavier than it did a minute ago.

Holding a bag of human bones and seeing more bones piled up on the roadside where children played was bizarre enough. But what was to come was to be a true test of courage for me.

Before we visited Rizalito's home, we had one more detour to take care of.

"I have to remove the skeleton of a man at his family's request. The bones will be shipped to USA where the family has migrated," Rizalito told me.

"Don't be scared," he added when he saw my expression.

The skeleton had been entombed since 1946. I did not want to imagine the state it was now in.

We stopped at a large double tomb. Using a crowbar, Rizalito pried open the stone sealing the tomb on the right.

I squatted beside Rizalito, taking shallow breaths as he carefully removed the stone to reveal a dark, mossy cavern that was empty except for a skeleton.

To my shock, Rizalito crawled right into the tomb and, using his bare hands, swept the skeleton to the front, where he began to remove the bones one by one.

"Will you help me?" he said.

Uneasy, I hesitated for a long moment.

Running through my desperate mind was the frightened thought: *Should I do this, should I do this?*

I was really, really scared. But if I did not help Rizalito, how would I understand what it was like to be in his shoes? If I did not do this, why was I here?

So with a prayer, I reached into the cavern with shaky hands and pulled out one bone, then another, and another with my bare fingers, placing each one carefully in a canvas bag.

When Rizalito pulled out the skull and handed it to me, I could see the teeth and the hair still attached to it. Steeling my will, I took the skull.

The moment I held that skull, my whole perspective of the job of an undertaker changed. An overwhelming feeling of fear turned into deep respect for Rizalito and his fellow caretakers.

I realised how sacred their job was. They looked after the dead to look after the living.

My terror at handling human bones with my bare hands turned into deep respect for cemetary caretakers like Rizalito, who look after the dead to look after the living.

This was not a job that most people would choose. But Rizalito performed his duties with such care that I could not help but respect him. In that instant, the role of a cemetery caretaker became transformed in my mind from a lowly job to one that had my utmost respect.

Rizalito had started helping his father in this line as a young boy of seven or eight and his own young son was now learning from him. Unemployment was high even outside the cemetery. This was an honest living and Rizalito was not the least bit ashamed of it. Who was I to look down on him?

In that instant, I realised that whether you are a cemetery caretaker like Rizalito, a teacher, a CEO, a cleaner, or a *karang guni* rag-and-bone man, fulfilment is not about how much you earn but how much value you see in what you do. And value is not determined by profession but by how much you respect yourself and your job.

***

Still in wonder over what I had just done, I hurried after Rizalito as he led the way to Street 38.

"This is my home," he said with pride as we rounded a corner.

Like many other homes in the cemetery, his was actually a whitewashed mausoleum. Upper class mausoleums are grand with ornate gates, interior stone carvings and brilliant stained glass windows. Entire families are entombed within these chambers. Caretakers and their families often live in the mausoleum they care for, with the blessing of the owners.

In the yard, a chorus of cheerful quacks welcomed us as Rizalito said, "These are my *bibi*," waving towards two white ducks waddling over.

"These are my dogs," he nodded at some mongrels.

The way in which he introduced his home and family, showing off his ducks and his dogs, was endearing to me. He did not have much, but whatever he had meant something to him.

Walking through a heavy, red door, I saw the words *Lopez Fajardo* carved over it — the name of the family that owned the mausoleum.

Claustrophobic — not to mention superstitious — folks may have felt uncomfortable inside. There were no windows, only tombs and cold, stone shelves. But Rizalito's family had added cosy touches to their macabre home — a clock hung on the wall, a small fan rotated near a cot, and a few plates and pots sat on the shelf that functioned as their kitchen.

Rizalito had been the caretaker of this mausoleum his whole life, inheriting the job from his mother, who had passed away just a few months ago.

Susana Ranoco had been born in the Manila North Cemetary in 1931 and had lived the 82 years of her life within its walls. Rizalito had also been born here, as had his wife and two children.

He was one of the lucky ones. Many squatters who lived in the cemetery did not have a proper roof over their heads, living hand to mouth by earning a few pesos bearing funeral coffins by day and sleeping on tombstones in the open at night.

Still, a mausoleum is not designed to be a home. And the one Rizalito's family lived in had no running water — showers were taken at a public tap where residents also collected water in large jerry cans for cooking.

Rizalito's wife Ophelia cooked her meals over a portable gas stove in the yard. The family was cheerful as we gathered at a foldable table outdoors to share a lunch of rice and luncheon meat fried with egg. As we talked, I discovered that even this simple meal could not be taken for granted. About twice a week, if money was scarce, the family went hungry.

Gazing at chubby Morris who obviously loved his food, I could not imagine how I would feel as a mother if I had to let my child go hungry.

Caretaking this mausoleum provided them with a home of sorts but did not pay enough to put food on the table. So Rizalito also looked after

25 tombstones on the grounds, sweeping the leaves away and cleaning the stones.

***

When Rizalito left for work, I seized the opportunity to have a word with Ophelia, a round-faced 40 year old with a dimpled smile.

"Are you happy here?" I asked her off camera. To my surprise, she burst into tears.

"Oh no," I thought in dismay. "Maybe her husband has been ill treating her!"

But her reply took me by surprise.

The mausoleum that Rizalito's family calls home.

> *Fulfilment is not about how much you earn but how much value you see in what you do.*

"I am very, very happy," Ophelia said with shining eyes. "Even though we don't have much, as long as the family is together, I am contented with life. My husband, he is very responsible. He does his best to put food on the table."

"Do you love him?" I asked her frankly, woman to woman.

"I love him very much," she said bashfully.

Like Rizalito, Ophelia had been born and raised in this cemetery. She and her husband had met as youngsters when she was caretaking one tomb and Rizalito another. When they grew up, they had decided to get married.

To Ophelia, the cemetery was far from the depressing place that most people would imagine — this was where Rizalito's mother had found a job that could feed her children and raise her son to be the gentleman that Ophelia fell in love with.

Who would have guessed that such a place as a cemetery would have so much positivity? Where a boy could meet a girl and go on to have a happy family? After this, I learnt never to jump to conclusions — there is a story behind every face and every place.

***

I had a soft spot for Rizalito's young son Morris who, whenever he could, would be snacking on chocolate or ice-cream or a sweet bun. He was equal parts mischievous and mature. When his father called for him, Morris would come running on chubby legs, clutching his snack in one hand and his father's broom in the other.

We played Follow the Leader as Morris hopped from one tomb to another, leading me to an elevated spot in the cemetery where we could gaze over the treetops.

Left: Rizalito and his son, Morris, clean a 100-year-old mausoleum in time for the Festival of Undas. Right: A simple lunch of egg and luncheon meat is considered a scrumptious treat for the family.

"So Morris, what is it like for you living here?" I asked him.

"I like it!" he replied. "I'm not afraid of dead people — they won't steal your things like living people!"

"Do you want to be like your father when you grow up?"

"Yes," he replied without hesitation. "I want to work hard like my father. That's how I will have food to eat."

Watching Rizalito with his son, I could understand why Morris looked up to his father. Rizalito was the model of diligence and reliability. He spoke to his son firmly but calmly, gently correcting him when he was wayward.

Education has nothing to do with wisdom, I realised. Here was an uneducated man whom many would consider to be low on the social ladder. But, to me, he was a fine example of a wise father and loving husband.

***

The next day the whole of the Philippines was celebrating Undas, All Souls Day. The cemetery took on a carnival-like atmosphere.

Ten-year-old Morris won over our whole crew with his cheeky smile. Whenever we bought ourselves a drink or a sweet bun, we would buy an extra one for Morris.

Caretakers diligently swept the area and put a fresh coat of paint on tombstones. Streamers hung from trees. Vendors hawked flowers and drinks and suckling pig.

Families, some travelling here from other provinces, came by the droves with picnic baskets, mats, deck chairs, transistor radios and guitars, prepared to camp the night around their relatives' tombs.

Rizalito gave me a tour of the "best-dressed" tombs — one of the fancy mausoleums was alight with many-candled chandeliers and festooned with fresh grapes specially flown in from Holland for the occasion.

Another one had been built in 1913. Heaving open a wooden trapdoor on the ground, Rizalito revealed a dank subterranean cavern. During the Second World War, the family members who owned this mausoleum had hidden from the Japanese in here, he told me. Ironically, their lives had been saved by their mausoleum.

Most families gathered around simpler concrete tombs. They laid out their mats, chatting and singing the night away.

Living in the cemetery, without the opportunity to attend school, has not stopped Morris from aspiring to be a television newscaster when he grows up.

My heart was warmed by the sight of how much family meant to the Filipinos. Whether they gathered in grand mausoleums or around bare tombs, they were here to honour their departed family members. This was a yearly celebration of a life well lived by the people who had loved them.

How comforting it is to the living to know that when they depart, their family members will remember them and spend time with them at the cemetery year after year.

This year's Undas was special for Rizalito's family as it was the first time they were remembering his mother, who had passed on just a few months before.

The family set candles around her simple tombstone. All around us we could hear other families whiling the night away companionably.

"Mama loved Rizalito a lot," said his older sister who used to take care of him as a boy when their mother was busy. "Once he was playing with candles and burnt his ear. I did not dare let my mother know. I took him far away so he could cry without Mama hearing!"

The family laughed as I teased Rizalito about how naughty he was.

"My mother was an outstanding woman," Rizalito said. "As his son, I want to make her proud by doing a good job as a caretaker. She taught me everything."

The annual Festival of Undas sees tombs being spruced up and a carnival-like atmosphere descending upon the cemetery.

That night was very special to me. We had nothing with us, not even drinks. All we did was sit on the ground in the candlelight, looking at a picture of Rizalito's mother, talking about life and sharing the occasional joke. Yet I felt that it was time well spent.

I never knew that the living and the dead could live side by side. When my Godpa passed away, I visited his niche regularly for two months. I would sit in front of his picture and chat with him, saying, "Godpa, I miss you. This is what is happening in my life. What do you think?"

He had been a man full of wisdom who had always had a listening ear for me whenever I needed advice. Even after he passed on, I felt that his spirit was with me. It brought me comfort just to know that we were in the same space.

So I understood why the Filipinos celebrate Undas the way they do, taking their entire family, even the babies, to honour their loved one. When these little babies grow up they, too, will keep the tradition of honouring their parents and grandparents.

During the entire time I had been filming this episode, my family never left my mind. I had learnt so much about the meaning of family. I could not wait to go home.

When I had first been told of this assignment, I had been shown photos of a dilapidated, rather spooky-looking place. Although there was some trepidation, I had come here with an open mind. But I really did not expect to learn such precious values in a cemetery.

Isn't it amazing what we can learn from the humblest of people and circumstances?

> *Isn't it amazing what we can learn from the humblest of people and circumstances?*

Top: Nicholas's team of Kenyan Riders, whose dream it is to one day compete in the Tour de France. Bottom: A young man patches up an old bicycle, which he hopes will see him to the finish line in a race organised by Nicholas.

kenya

NICHOLAS: FROM KATONG TO KENYA

On a rugged slope in the highlands of the African Rift Valley, a simple sign, handwritten, perched on the side of a road that wound relentlessly uphill.

The sign read:

RIDE A BLACK MAMBA BICYCLE
FROM BIRETWO TO TAMBACH CHATHOLIC (sic) CHURCH
IN UNDER 34 MIN
TO WIN KSH 200.000
CYCLIST MUST BE BORN BETWEEN 1990 & 1996

A clutch of bicycles and their riders milled about on the grass verge in a buzz of pre-race activity.

An orange bicycle was having some screws tightened. A seat, perhaps from a borrowed bicycle, was being lowered. Some tape was being wound around a worn-out tyre as a makeshift bandage. A bicycle rolled by, the step

Left: A row of Black Mamba bicycles awaiting the start of the race.
Right: Ghichora leads as the exciting race winds uphill.

of one pedal missing, leaving only a naked spindle.

The riders were young, their bikes not so much.

On a previous race, one of the bicycles did not even have brakes and the rider had slowed its downhill hurtle with his foot, causing a stream of smoke to rise from his sneaker.

Still, for many of these boys, this was not their first attempt at the race. The grand prize of KES 200,000, about S$3,000, could buy a piece of land here in Iten.

So far no one had yet won the KES 200,000 prize for completing this 11km stretch with a climb of 700m within 34 minutes, although 19-year-old Joseph Gichora had fallen short by just 43 seconds in the last race.

Added to the challenge was the fact that each boy had to race in a clunky Black Mamba, an "uncle bike" with a frame about 17 times heavier than that of a racing bike.

"You have to be superman to do this!" I said incredulously, gazing at the motley group of boys, many of whom didn't even have helmets.

"Yup, that's what these guys are," said Nicholas Leong with the proprietory air of a proud father.

Australian cycling coach Simon Blake, hanging near the back of the pack, a Go-pro strapped to his helmet, thundered out some final words of advice. "Good luck today. As you know, don't go too hard too early. I hope someone gets the money."

Young hopefuls, hungry in more ways than one, getting ready to vye for the race prize of S$3,000.

Nicholas handed me a red flag. "You can flag them off," he said.

I was absolutely thrilled. Giving the flag a mighty wave, I shouted, "GO!"… and then "Go, go, go, GO!" as a dozen bikes tore past me.

Scrambling into the back of a van with its back door open, I sat with Nicholas, the organiser of the race, and cheered the cyclists on as we pulled ahead, driving in front of the pack.

"GO, GICHORA, GO!" Nicholas and I yelled out to the front runner, hoping that he could scythe 43 seconds off his race time.

The steep climb was brutal. The riders' faces were expressionless masks of concentration, but their twitching muscles gleamed with the sweat of their exertion.

"Look, the only guys who are going to fight for this are Tony and Gichora," commentated Nicholas for my benefit.

Alongside us, another cruising car was full of boys waving the red flag and hanging out of the windows to cheer their friends on.

"Tony is right behind!" I said as I redoubled my cheers for Gichora. His strength flagging and confidence leaking, Gichora was nervously stealing backward glances.

Pumping hard at his pedals, Tony drew alongside Gichora and the two were grinding at their bikes, neck and neck.

"This is a RACE!" shouted Nicholas.

"Tony has caught up with him!" I yelled back, clutching Nicholas's arm.

Top: Plucked from obscure jobs like shoeshining, *boda-boda* bicycle-taxi driving and cattle herding, the riders now dream of competing in the most famous race in the world: the Tour de France. Bottom: Nicholas is a big brother to the riders, each of whom he has hand-picked.

This was much more exciting than I had ever expected an amateur race to be. For the last few days Nicholas had been telling me about his dream of fielding the world's first black African team to the Tour de France, and I had caught the enchantment of his dream.

One of these boys pushing up the hill in front of me could be the new Lance Armstrong!

***

My camera crew and I had flown to Kenya in 2012 to look up Singaporean Nicholas Leong, then 44. He had set up his dream team: a 15-man cycling corps living and training together with the goal of one day taking on the Tour de France.

Nick lived in a low, brick home with a thin, metal door that went *klong klong* when we knocked.

A burly man with dark eyes and a disarming smile, he shook our hands and asked, "Was my house very hard to find?"

"Yes!" I mock complained. Africans did not seem to believe in putting up street names. Or house numbers. And we had found Nicholas with some difficulty.

"Well, this is Kenya," he said cheerfully, as though that explained it all.

Contrasting with the natural abundance of trees and shrubs outside his house, the inside of his living room was a computer-driven control room, with a laptop, printer, cameras and gadgets everywhere, proving that you can take a guy out of the city but you can't take the city out of a guy.

The techy toys were perhaps one of the few links he had to Singapore here in Iten, which in many ways is as far removed from Singapore as it can be.

The story of how Nick came to be in Iten is pretty madcap.

He had been watching the 2006 Standard Chartered Marathon in Singapore when he noticed that out of the first 15 runners who crossed the line, 13 were Kenyans. An inspired thought crossed his mind: If sub-Saharan Africans dominated marathons and they had the same physique and aerobic capacity as professional cyclists, what's to stop a black African team from winning the crown of cycling races: the Tour de France?

Buying a plane ticket to Nairobi for the next night on a hunch that the Kenyans would be heading homeward, he introduced himself to Amos Matui, who had won the marathon, and told him, "I'm following you home!"

Home turned out to be high-altitude Iten, overlooking the Great Rift Valley, a remote town with an official population of just 4,000 but a disproportionate number of world-class athletes, including several Olympic gold medallists, middle- and long-distance world record setters and elite marathoners. Roughly a quarter of the population were athletes, honing their endurance and aerobic skills on steep slopes 2,400m above sea level.

Like a star-struck schoolboy, Nick found it "incredible to be in such a nondescript-looking town, have a chat with a passing guy and find out that he's a two-time world marathon champion".

A commercial photographer by profession, Nick had been hit by an epiphany of sorts.

"When I was in my late 30s I thought, 'Everything I'd ever done in life would have happened if I didn't do it. Every photo shoot that I'd ever done would have gone on without me. Every ad campaign that I'd ever done would have gone on without me.' I wanted to do something that wouldn't have happened if I hadn't started it. This is not a judgement on anybody else. It's just how I feel I should be using my life and the years I've been given."

Running parallel to that plot was the fact that Nick was an avid Tour de France fan.

Kamariny stadium, with its plain dirt track, has produced many a world champion marathoner.

"When I was a teenager, there was a bike shop near my secondary school, St Patrick's, called Ah Boon's Bikes. I walked into it one day and I still remember those beautiful bikes in the shop. There were these lovely 1970s posters of the Tour de France. They looked like tough guys, and I told myself that this was a sport that I would follow. I guess I've been hooked ever since."

Everything the Katong boy knew about cycling was gleaned from years of watching telecasts of Tour de France.

"I'm like the guy who sits there on Saturday and watches Manchester United and has watched Manchester United for 30 years, so he thinks he knows everything about the game," he said with good humour.

Putting two and two together, he decided to start a professional cycling team: Kenyan Riders. That he had neither been to Kenya before he followed Amos Matui home, nor worked in professional cycling circles, were of paltry significance to the irrepressible Nick.

He credits his mother for his sense of adventure and perseverance. Angela Leong, 79, was one of the first visually handicapped people to find employment as a switchboard operator in the 1950s.

"My mother told me that pioneers have it harder," Nick said. "Whatever they try to do has never been done and most people need to see something to believe it. They don't believe in what you're doing and they don't believe in you. So, you have to believe in yourself."

The town of Iten in the African Rift Valley, dubbed the "home of champions".

***

In his radical way of getting things done, Nick's recruitment process was, in his own words, "eclectic". He approached *boda-boda* cyclists who made a living ferrying people in their bicycle-taxis and, with a stopwatch in hand, would pay them to haul his 100kg frame up the hill. The fastest of the lot was Samwel Mwangi.

We visited Mwangi's home one morning. Up a dirt path and through a doorway that was no more than a rectangle cut out of a solid zinc sheet, we came to a compound of low, single storey buildings with cinder-block walls. A row of doors marked different homes and we stopped at a green door the colour of unripe plaintains. Outside sat a youthful looking lad with the glossy ebony skin and handsome cheekbones of the Kikuyu tribe. He was bouncing a baby on his knee.

"This is Mwangi," Nicholas introduced as Mwangi extended a hand in greeting.

"You look really young and you have a kid already?" I exclaimed.

"I have three!" he laughed softly, a beautiful smile wreathing his face.

He led us into his home, and we sat on two small sofas in the modest living room.

"So how did you meet?" I asked Nick.

"I wanted to see if he was a strong guy 'cos he went for a race and he was kind of okay but he wasn't the best. I thought he had potential. So I sat in his *boda-boda* and said, 'Look, I'll pay you 35 shillings to take me up that hill.'"

"What?" I looked from Nick's bulky frame to Mwangi's lean one. Nick was twice the man Mwangi was… literally.

"How much is that in Singapore currency?"

"About 50 cents," replied Nick with a chuckle. "But his normal fare is 20 shillings, and I paid him 35… almost twice that!"

Mwangi grinned good naturedly.

"Mwangi was one of the first people I met," said Nick. "He had talent, so I said, 'I'll take you to France and I'll take you up this mountain and the greatest cyclist that's ever lived did it in 37 minutes. Let's see how close you're going to get.'"

Mwangi and his baby in the house that he acquired with his earnings as a Kenyan Rider.

> *They don't believe what you're doing and they don't believe in you. So, you have to believe in yourself.*

Nick took Mwangi and another rider he found in nearby Eldoret, shoeshine Zakayo Nderi, to Alpe d'Huez, the most celebrated leg of the Tour de France. The night before the climb, Nderi dreamt of slaying a lion. The next morning the two riders, uncoached and inexperienced, bolted up the 21 famous hairpins in 42 and 43 minutes.

It was a resounding affirmation of their raw talent and enough for Kenyan Riders to find financial backers in Matthieu and Marie-Anne Vermersch. The French couple has been Kenyan Riders' investor since.

Mwangi and Nderi were offered positions in Kenyan Riders that came with training and a stable income. Two months ago, Mwangi's family of five moved out of derelict living conditions and into this new home, which Mwangi described appreciatively as having a "better living environment".

"Has Nick's presence, his friendship, changed your life?" I asked.

"He is like a father to me," said Mwangi simply.

Watching Nick's face, I saw the tough-guy demeanor crack a little.

"Is this the first time you've heard this?" I asked.

"Yeah," Nick said, a little embarrassed by his emotion. "Over here in Africa people don't express themselves much. Maybe it's a male thing as well, who knows. But… it's gratifying. It's really gratifying. I mean, this is why I'm here."

The next morning, we had breakfast with his riders and coach Simon.

In a modest room at the training centre, the riders sat at several wooden tables chugging juice from great mugs and chomping down bananas and *chapattis* studded with vegetables and meat, skillet-fried by the team's cook.

There was an air of brotherhood as they joshed about and ate together.

"Simon is the coach, he has to be here with you," I said to the boys. "But why does Nick have to have breakfast with you every morning?"

"He's our father, and family has to be here. He has to be here to look after his children," quipped one of the riders.

"Wow, Nick, you have 15 kids!" I teased him as the boys laughed.

Simon wrapped a banana in a *chapatti* — his happy meal.

"May I try that?" I asked, biting into the *chapatti-burrito*. It was delicious — both sweet and salty and a real energy pack for the boys who trained for full days.

Mwangi was a *boda-boda* bicycle-taxi cyclist when Nicholas talent-scouted him by having Mwangi take him up the hill as fast as possible.

"So do you like being a part of Kenyan Riders?" I asked the boys.

"We love it," came the reply. "It is our career now. We don't do it because of Nick, we do it because of ourselves."

Out among the trees, Simon and Nick had carved out a mountain biking trail and after breakfast the boys rode the trail with vigour. It looked like fun.

"Yeah, the mountain bike session are quite enjoyable," said Simon. "Skills come through play. Here they're building a really good relationship with their bicycles. One of the biggest challenges is trying to think like an African and trying to think how an African would benefit the most in cycling but doing it their own way."

Several riders were speed pedaling on bikes that were hiked up on stationary blocks, turning the garden into an outdoor spinning class.

For the first time in their lives, the riders are properly kitted up.

A few others were cycling, nose to tail, around and around the sides of a small dirt bowl carved out of the terrain. One lost his concentration and stuttered to a stop, causing the rest to crash into each other and tumble like human dominoes into the dirt with a general shout of laughter.

But when I saw the entire team cycle in a fluid peloton on an uphill road, I drew a sharp breath. Gone was the boyish buffoonery. It was a beautiful thing to watch them move, as slender as their bikes were sleek, an inborn poise in their form. Despite their professional-looking kit, there was nothing cosmetic about them, they were all natural muscle and sinew and grace.

"We can't import Western methods into Kenya. This is not possible, because this is Africa and every programme that has ever been designed in cycling has been designed for westerners," said Nick.

The Kenyan Riders in training.

"What we're developing is really unique. We look different and we'll train differently and we'll race differently and we'll be a team that's going to dazzle. Hopefully."

***

In the early days of the project, around 2009 before he secured the Vermerschs' financial backing, Nick had not completely given up commercial photography as he was worried about dwindling finances. He chose to shuttle between Kenya and Singapore, working alternately on Kenyan Riders and photo shoots.

The turning point came when he was in the north of Kenya, where a large number of marginalised Turkana tribesman lived.

"I had a hunch that they might be as equally talented as the (dominant) Kalenjin and Kikuyu tribes and could use the opportunity I hoped Kenyan Riders could provide," said Nick.

So for three months he lived in the hot, semi-arid north that was prone to drought and widespread hunger. Tribal feuds over cattle were common.

Life in Kenya is often a struggle for survival, making stable work a matter of life and hope for families.

"In one of the cattle raids, a young woman died and her husband's family asked me to take her body back to her home in another village, which I did," he said. "Within 55 hours of sending her body back to her village, I found myself sitting in an ad agency in Singapore, listening to a creative person complaining about a pink blouse and asking my opinion as a photographer. I remember saying something that sounded reasonable, but thinking: *No, I can't do this. I can't.* That was when I left my career and went off to live in Kenya full-time."

***

Despite capturing the world's imagination by regularly churning out champions, Iten still grappled with the spectre of poverty. Many of the athletes were driven by the desire to escape the hardship of life here.

Thirteen-year-old Isaac Koech, who won a 2km race organised by the London Marathon for schoolchildren in 2012, told reporters, "I like to run, but I want to be rich one day from running and build a big home."

He had won the race without shoes.

His family lived adjacent to bean and maize fields just outside of Iten. Some slept in the bare mud huts common in the province.

Nick was convinced that Kenyans had the talent "to go to the very top of the industry" and make a living for themselves in cycling. They had already done that with running. They just lacked a platform in cycling.

"That is our role: To provide them with opportunity that cuts across social disparities," said Nick.

"People in poor countries do not exist to give richer people a teaching moment," he added wryly. Kenyan Riders was giving them a livelihood that they had to earn for themselves, it was not charity.

His riders came from remarkable backgrounds.

John Njoroge had been a milkman, waking up at 5am every morning to deliver 50 litres of milk on a rickety bike.

Suleiman Kangangi was a Kikuyu tribesman who, as a young boy, had taught himself to read and write and speak English despite being hired out by his family as a cattle herdsman.

Young trainee Geoffrey Panyako was a *boda-boda* cyclist who had acquired a reputation in the team as one of the toughest competitors. Once he cycled 480km over two days on his Black Mamba to arrive in Iten at 3am, whereupon he ate a few *chapattis,* went to sleep and showed up for a race at 8am, finishing sixth in a grueling climb.

"All of our riders are good guys. What I'm sure of is that if they were born in another country or another continent, they would definitely have more opportunities than they have now," said Nick.

Each was provided with food, lodging, equipment and a monthly stipend of S$220 to S$380, a decent wage above the national average, which helped them feed their families and educate their children.

"Hopefully the members of the team have had their lives changed for the better," said Nick. "They all draw a salary. Some of them have bought small plots of land from prize money from races. Hopefully, when we turn into a professional team, their lives will improve even more."

***

In the morning, Nick took me on one of his visits to a few secondary schools where he was trying to create awareness of cycling as a sport.

Fresh-faced schoolboys gathered around us at the schools which were set on a hilltop overlooking the vast African vista.

"All those who can run 5km below 15 minutes, you come in front," instructed a schoolteacher. A good number stepped forward.

"This gives us an idea of their aerobic capacity, their endurance capability," Nick told me.

"What is your time?" he asked the boys.

"14:17," said a boy with a serious mien and a direct gaze.

"14:17 is seriously fast for a schoolboy," Nick laughed a little and shook his head in disbelief. "The world record is 12:37. Really world class is 13 minutes. They're only lagging behind by 1 minute. And they're not even trained."

He addressed the boys. "Who wants to train for bicycle racing?"

The younger children looked blank, some older ones at the back raised a hand.

Nick organised the Black Mamba School Race Series to encourage greater use of the bicycle so that those living far away could still attend school.

Nicholas organises races at secondary schools to test the boys' aerobic capacity.

"Who wants to train for bicycle racing?" Nicholas asks a crowd of schoolboys.

Kenyan Riders was also planning to work with more bicycle NGOs and award full cycling scholarships to deserving students. After high school, talent spotted boys would be invited to join the seniors and earn an apprentice salary.

Kenyan Riders' philosophy was to use local resources, starting with the heavy, single-speed Black Mamba commonly used in Kenya for transportation and to earn a livelihood. The boys were not given racing bikes until much later.

"We want to delay the giving of the professional bicycle so that they can actually develop a culture based on the resources that they already have," explained Nick, revealing the thoughtfulness with which he has constructed the programme.

***

The day that Tony and Gichora raced up the hill for the KES 200,000 prize was the day I truly caught Nick's vision, felt it in my gut.

It was Gichora's eyes that did it. He was pulling up the hill just a few metres from our car as Nick and I cheered him on.

I could see the raw determination that bordered on desperation in his eyes as he pushed through his agony to reach the finish line.

"Gichora, C'MON, Tony's right behind you!" I yelled.

Tony pumped hard and drew alongside Gichora. And then… passed him, sailing across the finish line.

He had made it in 35 minutes, just one minute short. The prize money would not be given out today.

Ghichora strains to finish the grueling race within the stipulated time, but falls short by a gut-wrenching three minutes.

Instead t-shirts were presented to each participant as their timing was called out. The smiling boys didn't look too devastated. With their old, single-speed bikes that were missing pedals and brakes, they had known that this was a long shot. They would try again next time.

The day after the race, Nick took me along with him on a visit to Gichora. Past a green field and copse of slender trees, we followed a dirt path and came to a clearing where a few mud huts were scattered. The clearing was utterly barren — no crops grew in the knobbly cow grass, no animals were to be seen.

Gichora held open a wooden plank door as we entered his hut. He smiled as he shook our hands, a handsome, tall boy with his equally lanky younger brother in tow.

There was nothing in the house except for four mud walls, a dirt floor and a zinc roof overhead. I mean nothing. Not a single stick of furniture, not one scrap of belonging. There was no running water or electricity or cooking

Wildly cheering the riders past the finish line.

facilities. Off the single room was a tiny space with a single mattress covered by a green mosquito net. Gichora had four younger brothers and sisters. His parents were alcoholic and did not work. That one mattress appeared to be the only possession they had.

We sat on the dirt floor and leaned against the mud walls.

"Joseph Gichora is 19 and he just finished primary school last year," Nick told me by way of introduction.

"What do you do here every day?" I asked Gichora, trying to draw him into conversation.

He cast about for an answer and, finding none, offered a shy smile instead.

"Nothing," Nick gently answered for Gichora. "There's nothing to do here. The land is not theirs, so they can't even plant crops."

Top: The only prizes given out that day are t-shirts, yet the boys remain endearingly cheerful. Bottom: Ghichora and his bare, mud-walled home.

"Where do you find the food for your family?" Nick asked him.

"Buy. From the shop," Gichora said.

"Where do you get the money to buy?" Nick asked.

Gichora tried to find the words. "My mother is hustling to get the money."

We fell silent as I struggled with my emotions. I understood now why despite Gichora's determination and raw power, he could not get up the hill in 34 minutes — he hardly had anything to eat.

"Gichora, we have to think about a solution for you," Nick interjected rather sternly. He had met Gichora when the boy was 15 and had seen his potential. But this was an extremely poor family, he had told me earlier. After primary school, Gichora's parents had not been able to afford to send him to secondary school and his future was bleak. His only hope lay in cycling.

"Now you're not training properly, that's the problem," said Nick. "Do you have a training programme?"

Silence.

"You need a training programme."

To my surprise, Nick's business-like manner softened and he teared.

"It's my job to choose," he mumbled softly to himself.

If he chose Gichora, he would not be able to give a job to Tony. If he gave the position to Tony, he would have to reject Gichora. It was a wrenching decision. Either way, someone would lose out on a different life, a different destiny.

Finally, looking into Gichora's eyes, Nick said, "You're strong, you're young. You should come in."

Gichora gave a hint of a smile, hardly daring to believe what he thought he had heard.

"So, it's done? You've decided? He's in?" I said, starting to hop up and down in glee.

"Yeah," Nicholas cracked a boyish grin. "He's got a lot of endurance and he could really go somewhere. He's got a perfect climber's physique and we have a lot of hope in him."

I was so happy for Gichora, I pumped the poor boy's hand up and down wildly. And Nick — I had new insight into this big, tough guy. Inside, he was just a softie.

***

When Nick had spoken of how he could not spend the rest of his life considering the merits of a pink blouse, I felt deeply ashamed. That was exactly the life I was living — work, family, what to wear, what to eat. That was how I passed my days.

He made me question what I was doing with my life and the numbered days I had. Could I do more?

Ultimately Nick's goal was not just to groom a group of professional cyclists but to provide opportunities for them to one day make good and give back to their own community.

All the glowing press write-ups about the athletic potential of Kenyan Riders missed the point. There was a bigger picture, a bigger dream, than Tour de France.

"It takes courage to do what my riders are doing," Nick said to me.

I think it also takes courage for him to do what he is doing: To invest in people. To dream big.

***

Two years later...
Nick was in Singapore in 2014 publicising Kenyan Riders when he received the kind of phone call no one is ever prepared to receive.

John Njoroge Muya, their star cyclist, had been killed in an accident while the team was racing in the Tour of Matabungkay in the Philippines. Njoroge was in the lead when a car, which had repeatedly ignored road marshals' warnings to stop, collided head-on into the 30 year old as he went round a bend downhill at approximately 100kmh.

Kenyan Riders coach Rob Higley guessed that he had made a split second decision not to swerve away from the car as he would have endangered the safety of the other cyclists.

Njoroge's tragic death, while he was proudly wearing his first yellow jersey, shook the entire African racing community. At his funeral, thousands

The faces of future champions. Any one of these children in Iten could grow up to be a world record holder.

from all over Kenya came to honour this special man who five years ago had been an obscure bicycle courier delivering milk.

"I was attending a friend's wedding at the time when the coach called me with the news. I couldn't process the details," recalled Nick soberly.

"The thing that was hard about his death was because of the unlikeliness of how we met. He was from this very small, nondescript African hamlet. It's a place where nothing tragic really happens and nothing good really happens so you live in this airless parochialism — you know exactly who you're going to marry, you know how many kids you're going to have, you know who's going to bury you when you die. It's fine for a lot of people but if you're John Njoroge, you have these dreams of being a professional cyclist. So for me to have found him, and for him to have found me, it was absolutely unlikely. Because of that, I was convinced that we were going to get to the Tour de France together."

Nick flew to the Philippines on the very day of the accident to take Njoroge back to his village and his widow.

"Thousands came to honour and respect the man and the achievements of his short life because he was a very special person. In the short time he was with us he became the best cyclist in Kenya and he became a hero of sorts for lots of people."

While shaken by their teammate's tragic departure, the riders continued on with their Asian tour and won other races.

"They could have abandoned the Asian campaign and gone home and we would not have judged them harshly. But none of them did. All of them wanted to finish it," said Nick. "The accident had strengthened their resolve. So it was very heartening.

"The people on our team have a vision for themselves to realise their full talent, to be somebody in the world, feed their family, inspire their community. After Njoroge, the risks have become palpable. But they still want to continue on this path we've set out on together. All of them have a story like Njoroge. All of them are living in obscurity and anonymity and have a vision for themselves but no outlet. Now that we've provided that outlet, they are holding on to it. It's very precious."

When Kenyan Rider John Njoroge, arguably the best cyclist in the country, died in a tragic cycling accident in the Philippines, thousands of Kenyans gathered to pay their respects.

A fund has been set up for Njogore's widow and one-year-old son. The whole team, all the way from the funders to the cyclists, the coaches, the cooks, and the trainees, have recommitted themselves to the project and mean to see their dream come to fruition on the inclines of the Tour de France.

As for Gichora, "he is a fantastically strong guy!" Nick said with a chuckle. He is still on the team today and as I write this, Gichora is in Europe at the Haute Route, competing in the tough amateur race that mimics all the stages of the Tour de France.

"He's still very young, only 21 or 22 years old. If he keeps his head he's going to be very, very good. We're hopeful for him... for the whole team," said Nick. "The recent revelations about doping during the Lance Armstrong era have cast a shadow on the sport. That's the unfortunate narrative we find ourselves with. We have a project that can potentially change that narrative."

We often think of change makers as the Steve Jobses, the Aung San Suu Kyis, the Barack Obamas. But in this case, the change makers are a milkman, a shoeshine, a cowherd. And one Singaporean with a big dream.

What change is waiting for you and me to make, I wonder.

> *We often think of change makers as the Steve Jobses, the Aung San Suu Kyis, the Barack Obamas. But in this case, the change makers are a milkman, a shoeshine, a cowherd. And one Singaporean with a big dream.*

Despite being stung by Ugandan "killer bees" thousands of times, Lesster has persisted in his Little Honey Man dream. He believes that Uganda is the last frontier where pure, unadulterated honey can be cultivated.

uganda

LESSTER: THE LITTLE HONEY MAN

When I was eight or nine years old, I was obsessed with the movie *Killer Bees*.

My family was not well off and we did not have a lot of entertainment at home, so I watched the movie again and again even though it freaked me out.

I remember vividly the part where some ill-advised person wandered into a forest and got attacked by a swarm of killer bees. In a scene that was a triumph of special effects, there was a close-up of the unfortunate victim's skin as the bees pierced the flesh and dramatically injected the poison. That scene succeeded in giving me a phobia of bees and nightmares for weeks.

So you can imagine how terrified I was to be wearing a bee suit in Uganda, about to face my biggest fear: African bees, the most aggressive in the world and the very creatures that had given rise to the ominous moniker of "killer bees".

***

Uganda is a land lush with grassy plains and undulating hills.

It was 2008 and my camera crew and I had flown 17 hours from Singapore to Dubai and then to Uganda in search of Singaporean Lesster Leow, 46, also known as The Little Honey Man.

Uganda, which sits on the equator, is a land lush with grassy plains and undulating, green hills. Its rivers, forests, lakes, hot springs, and national parks with exotic names like Bwindi Impenetrable Forest, draw ecotourists hoping to spot big game such as leopards, lions, hyenas, hippos, wildebeest, elephants, and even mighty gorillas. Lake Victoria, the second largest lake in the world and the source of the River Nile, is one of Uganda's jewels.

Sadly, the spectacular country has also suffered from decades of civil war in the 1970s and 1980s which took half a million lives. Ugandans, especially in the remote villages, are still struggling to recover from the social and economic trauma of war and personal loss.

I knew it was going to be meaningful to film in such an extraordinary country, so far removed from stable Singapore. But I had no idea just how special it would turn out to be.

***

As usual I only had a piece of paper to help me find my profile, and as I walked down the red mud road, I tried to follow the instructions: *Look for* the Mickey Mouse sign. Walk 300 metres, turn left at the fork. The house is the one with a green gate and a jackfruit tree outside.

All I could think of was, "*Hah?* Jackfruit tree? I'm a city girl, I don't know what a jackfruit tree looks like!"

The street was lush with wild trees of all kinds and I was thoroughly confused. Fortunately I knew a green gate when I saw one and after knocking loudly for a while, a square peephole slid open and a bespectacled eye appeared.

"Hello, are you Lesster?" I said.

"Yes, yes, come in," he said and pushed the gate open.

With his youthful, round face, Lesster immediately reminded me of Teamy, the Productivity Bee, from Singapore's National Productivity Board campaign of the 1980s.

"So this is where you live," I said with interest as Lesster showed me his brick, ranch-style house that sat on an acre of land fragrant with papaya and jackfruit trees, *kangkong*, sweet potato and chilli plants.

Cattle driven by herdsmen make a picturesque sight on the streets.

Four german shepherd guard dogs roamed the grounds: Jackie and Sammo, which he had named after Jackie Chan and Sammo Hung "because they are very aggressive, like kungfu masters", and Tammy, after a sweet-natured character in *Growing Up*, the popular MediaCorp television series of the 1990s.

A housekeeper, an accountant, a boy who helped with the honey refining, a goat that "ate everything but grass", and a good number of bees rounded up the residents in Lesster's little paradise.

Inside his house, rows of little honey jars attractively packaged in miniature clay huts sat on a shelf, ready to be delivered to a local supermarket. Hefty 25kg plastic tubs of honey were lined up against a wall, waiting to be exported to Zurich.

***

Seven years ago Lesster had left a lucrative job with an Indonesian company in Singapore to embark on a new adventure.

"I felt that I was halfway through my life and I had not really seen or done anything that was 'out of this world'," said Lesster. "I told myself, 'Why don't I do something interesting and new?'"

"But why Africa?" I asked him curiously.

"Africa is in many ways the last frontier," he replied. "It is a land of opportunity."

Lesster's idyllic new life in Uganda includes a ranch-style home complete with dogs and a mischievous goat that eats everything but grass.

Settling in Uganda with the intention of selling fire extinguishers, Lesster quickly discovered that things were not that simple.

"The country was so poor in 2001 that people could not even afford three meals a day, much less a fire extinguisher," Lesster said. "If their hut was on fire, it was cheaper for them to let their huts burn and rebuild them than to buy a fire extinguisher!"

Coincidentally, the Ugandan government was introducing honey farming as a viable source of income for its people, and invited Lesster to visit their bee keeping facilities and honey refinery.

Consulting with a German beekeeping expert, Lesster discovered that not only was there a worldwide shortage of 700,000 metric tonnes of honey, Uganda was an ideal place to cultivate honey as the land was still untainted by industrialisation, which meant that unadulterated honey of a high quality could be produced.

That was the start of The Little Honey Man brand.

Working with the local farmers to set up a network of a few hundred hives, Lesster started by producing 500kg of honey for distribution to a local supermarket. In Africa, honey is used for medicinal purposes.

He also struck a distribution deal with a wealthy Swiss banker who had set up an orphanage in Uganda and was looking for a Ugandan product to sell in Zurich to raise funds for the orphanage. Production eventually grew

Some of Lesster's bee boxes have a spectacular view of the Ugandan plains.

Lesster has declared himself immune to bee venom after being stung innumerable times!

to 8,000kg, which was the limit of Lesster's capacity as a one-man show.

***

Starting a business from scratch without experience can get you burnt. But in Lesster's case, it got him stung.

"When I first started in 2003, I knew nothing about beekeeping… *zero*," Lesster told me. "The German expert took me to the village to give me a practical lesson on working with bees. It was a painful experience because I was stung 40 times on my face and went into a one-and-a-half day coma."

"Forty times!" I exclaimed. "Was that the only time you've been stung?"

"No, I've been stung thousands of times," he replied matter of factly. "So much so that I've built up an immunity to the bee venom and don't even swell up when I get stung now."

Lesster was making me increasingly nervous… it was going to be my turn to face these very bees in a moment.

That day we had driven for hours across the Ugandan savannah to visit some of Lesster's bee farms in the west. I was about to face my childhood fears by having a close encounter with the bees.

Not only did scenes of the *Killer Bees* movie flash before my eyes, I also had a real and painful memory of being stung. During the filming of another travelogue, *Planet Shakers*, in Australia a few years earlier,

BELINDA LEE

I had been stung by a bee. The burning was excruciating, my body went hot and I developed a fever. Long after I had healed physically, I still carried the psychological scars within me.

So when Lesster helped me into the bee suit — loose, white overalls with thick gloves and a wide-brimmed hat trimmed with protective netting — I told him with a nervous laugh, "Must seal the Velcro properly, you know."

"African bees are some of the most aggressive in the world and they don't sting singly, they attack in swarms," Lesster said cheerfully, oblivious to the *kiasi*, frightened-to-death, expression on my face.

***

I approached the cluster of beehives so carefully that I looked like I was walking on the moon in my space suit.

Lesster handed me a smoker and showed me how to smoke the bees without burning them.

"The smoke simulates a forest fire and when this happens the bees return to the hive, start sucking on the honey and become more calm," he explained.

Lifting the zinc lid of the wooden hives, he revealed a row of wooden slats. Carefully he showed me how to lift one slat by holding both ends. Clinging to the underside was a magnificent honeycomb crawling with bees.

Even as I admired the bees' handiwork, my heart was going *pip-pop pip-pop*. I hardly dared to move and did not want to speak loudly for fear

You mean I have to face killer bees? Yes, I was terrified! This little fella even ambushed me in the car where I was hiding from its mates.

Filming at one of Lesster's bee farms, where I snapped this photo in a hurry before I sought refuge in the car.

that the bees would start attacking. When a few wayward bees started buzzing around, I said very slowly, "Oh no. They. Are. Starting. To. Come out. How?"

"It's okay," said Lesster calmly. "You're doing well. Very good."

His composure was reassuring. He taught me how to gently brush away the bees from the honeycomb and saw the honeycomb off with a knife.

As we worked, he pointed out to me the queen bee and the amazing organisation of the bee colony. He showed me how honeycombs are one of the strongest structures in the world. Slowly my fear ebbed away as I became fascinated. I could see now why the art of beekeeping had completely captivated Lesster.

To my surprise, Lesster did not even wear gloves and headgear when working with his bees.

"I made the daring decision to shed my gloves when I realised that we are naturally more clumsy and careless when we wear gloves because psychologically we know that we are protected," said Lesster. "By removing my gloves I become gentler with the bees, which makes them calmer with me."

Through Lesster I learnt that honey bees generally live for only 40-odd days and one bee can only produce half a teaspoon of honey during its lifetime.

We eat honey by the spoonfuls. But how many of us spare a thought for the honeybees or what beekeepers go through to produce beautiful honey for our consumption?

"When I got my first beehive, I realised that African bees are no joke," he recounted. "I was wearing a bee suit when they started attacking me, but it was very frightening as they completely covered my suit and I could hear them stinging my protective gear. In fright, I banged the screen down — *BAM!* — and ran off.

"That day I killed so many innocent bees when they had done nothing to me. Once a bee stings you, it dies. So they wouldn't sting unless they feel threatened. I've come to understand that they are not the aggressors, they are just defending their home. I have learnt to respect them and understand how to work with them in a calm manner so that they don't lose their lives unnecessarily. Now when I get stung, I know that it is my fault and I think about how I could have handled things better. I've learnt to create a bond with the bees."

I had a newfound respect for honeybees and their courageous, knowledgeable beekeepers. Harvesting honey is not simply a matter of collecting it from the hives. It takes courage, experience, patience and sensitivity.

***

The next day we set off early for a long drive to the village of Gulu in northern Uganda — a journey of more than 330km. Lesster regularly drove hours to Gulu to share his beekeeping knowledge with the villagers.

Just one and a half years ago, the region around Gulu had been fraught with danger as the cult-like Lord's Resistance Army (LRA) had led a brutal, 20-year rebellion in Africa.

Top: The best part of filming with Lesster is getting to sample his freshly harvested honeycombs, some of which are fragranced with eucalyptus while others have a floral scent.
Below: Reminders of the devastation Gulu was subjected to during the brutal rebellion by the Lord's Resistance Army (LRA).

Thousands of villagers were viciously chopped down with machetes, swords and stones, and nearly 2 million northern Ugandans were displaced by the fierce fighting. The LRA became notorious for abducting up to 250,000 children to serve as soldiers and sex slaves. This led to a mass exodus of the northern Ugandans, who migrated in droves, to refugee camps further south.

"In 2006, the LRA was pushed back by the Ugandan army and driven off Uganda, and the district government was encouraging farmers to return to their abandoned villages," Lesster related. "Many of them were being housed in Internally Displaced Camps in the south and social problems were cropping up. So the solution was to have the farmers return to their northern villages and lead normal lives again.

"But the people were so poor, they did not even have money to buy seeds to plant crops. One of the ways they could start making an income was by beekeeping. They could cut natural rattan from the swamps and weave them into traditional beehives and eventually harvest the honey to sell. Once they have some money they can buy seeds for carrots, cabbage and maize. So to start them off with a skill is very important.

"If you give the locals money, they will spend it in a day. This is what war has taught them — that you live one day at a time. If I give them knowledge and skills, they will be able to help their family and community survive for a long time."

As we made our journey northwards, I saw that outside of Uganda's capital Kampala, people were still accustomed to walking everywhere.

We passed many villagers on foot, balancing a plastic tub or a bale of hay on their head, sometimes with a bag tied around their waist as well. What a practical way of carrying your belongings if you are walking a long distance!

We did not bring any food with us, so when we got hungry, we would stop the car and buy "satay sticks" of roasted meat from roadside stalls. I must have eaten at least half a dozen.

It was only seven years later when I met up with Lesster in Singapore to discuss this book that I discovered in a passing conversation with him what the "satay sticks" really were: skewered and roasted field rats! It was a free source of protein.

"Satay sticks" sold at roadside stalls. Was the meat chicken, mutton or, *gulp*, field rats? I will never know.

Just as well Lesster had not told me in Uganda what kind of satay I was eating or I might have gone on a hunger strike.

We passed villages where children were herding a few goats, cows and chickens, and farms surrounded by small plots of maize, tomatoes, cabbage and groundnuts.

The villages in the ravaged north were not so lucky.

We drove for hours down endless roads that sliced through the vast savannah until finally we arrived in Gulu.

Barbed wire and ominous signs that warned of land mines were reminders of the brutalisation this village had suffered in the past 20 years.

"The villagers tell me horrific stories of how the rebels would steal into their villages to kill, to rob and worst of all to kidnap their children who would be kept in the jungle and trained to become soldiers," said Lesster. "They tell me how they have seen the rebels put machine guns in children's hands and forced them to shoot their entire family. These children would leave the village from shame and would never be seen again."

Some of Lesster's own bee farmers had lost their children to the rebels.

Hearing about the savagery these poor villages had had to endure almost broke me.

But the Acholi villagers did not seem broken. As we walked through the village — a clutch of thatched roofed mud huts, some burnt and ransacked by rebels — we saw barefoot toddlers in tattered clothes cheerfully playing with dogs, mothers sitting outdoors peeling plaintains and boiling water on wood fires, older children carrying younger siblings on their hip. There was an air of contentment at having a place to call home, despite the impoverished state of their village.

About 150 men and boys gathered in a clearing, making themselves comfortable on logs or plastic chairs, surrounding Lesster as The Little Honey Man perched on a fallen tree trunk under a shady mango tree to share his beekeeping knowledge. A few mothers and children sat on the fringes of the group, ready for the afternoon's entertainment.

"I am a poor man," Lesster announced to the rapt listeners. "What I can give you is not money. But what I can give you is my knowledge. I can share with you how to keep bees. No magic. No *juju*. We borrow the bees' honey and when you look after them, they won't bite you or kiss you!"

The crowd chuckled. Some took notes with pen and paper, and I saw how earnest they were about learning.

Lesster's soft, humorous approach was adopted out of respect and thoughtfulness for the villagers.

"These people have lost hope and confidence in themselves as a result of the war," he told me. "As a *muzungu*, a foreigner, when I come to their homeland, I do not want to belittle them or patronise them. My approach is not to give them anything for free. They learn beekeeping and then they

Travelling on foot is common in Uganda, even if you have a harvest of plaintains to carry on your head.

Sharing honey-harvesting tips with the villagers.

have to practise it on their own. They will develop more self worth this way than from getting handouts."

Traditionally Ugandans were honey hunters, not beekeepers. They would set fire to a bunch of twigs and leaves, thinking they were smoking out the bees when in fact they were burning the bees. Not only did the bees get killed, the honey would be contaminated with ash. So Lesster shared with them improved methods of honey gathering.

The long drive to Gulu meant that Lesster sometimes stayed overnight with the villagers in their mud huts thatched with papyrus stalks. The toilets were pit latrines which Lesster was extra careful not to accidentally step into.

"I would eat what they eat — their favourite food in these parts is millet mixed with sand and made into balls," said Lesster. "Sometimes they would catch field rats and barbeque them… it was quite tasty!"

I was Lesster's assistant that day and as he demonstrated how to make beehives out of natural resources, I put aside squeamishness, even using my bare hands to seal logs with cow dung as instructed by Lesster.

"Don't worry," he reminded me, "cows only eat grass, so their dung is clean!"

The funny thing about my job is that I am constantly put in awkward, unpredictable situations and am called to do things that, given a choice, I would not do. But I realise now that this is the best form of education that I can ever receive.

***

"The Ugandans are a beautiful people — warm, generous and hospitable. On the road, they greet you even if you are a stranger," Lesster told me.

I experienced this hospitality for myself when we visited one of his beekeepers.

In a modest brick house surrounded by banana trees, the farmer's family had cooked up a feast for us. The entire table was covered with offerings of steamed fish, sweet potatoes, *posho* made from maize, and their staple food *matooke* or mashed plaintain.

The extended family of almost 20 people had been invited to dine with us, and they filled the small house, with the aunty, uncle, ah ma and ah kong sitting at the table with us and the younger children, wearing their best attire, sitting on the floor happily sharing food from one big platter.

I was overwhelmed by their hospitality. Fish and meat were reserved for special occasions and they had cooked everything in their kitchen in our honour.

We thanked them in the only way we knew how — by tucking into the food with relish.

Another memorable meal, although for different reasons, was at the Kingfisher Lodge, a rustic resort owned by Lesster's German friend Hans Fischer. The lodge had a scenic view of the vast Queen Elizabeth National Park and the Rwenzori mountain ranges.

When Lesster had first arrived in Uganda, bemused by the African culture and frustrated with the corruption that plagued business dealings, he was exploring the country in his car one day when he chanced upon the Kingfisher Lodge. There he met Mr Fischer and although they hailed from different parts of the world, they recognised in each other a kindred spirit.

"Mr Fischer had been living in Uganda for 15 or 20 years before me, and he told me, 'You cannot expect Uganda to be like Singapore. Slow down, take one or two steps back, and really understand the African culture instead of trying to force your own culture on the locals.' That was a turning point for me," recalled Lesster.

That evening, with a view of a watercolour sunset over the African savannah, Mr Fischer threw an extravagant barbeque for us, replete with grilled meat, fish, sweet potato and vegetables. We ended the evening by dancing exuberantly to the rhythm of traditional African drums and bells. I even managed to persuade Lesster to do the local dance for the first time — a kind of congo line with energetic foot stomping and plenty of booty shaking!

***

The film crew poses with longtime Ugandan resident, Mr Fischer (second from right), at the Kingfisher Lodge overlooking the rolling grasslands of Queen Elizabeth National Park.

Traditional dancers shake up a storm at the Kingfisher Lodge.

Back in Kampala, Lesster took me to his regular lunch spot — a small shack with a zinc roof, and a sign declaring:

Food Point
For delicious meals

There was just one small table outside and a few plastic chairs. We sat down and talked undisturbed for a long time until, puzzled, I asked, "Does the waitress know that we're here?"

Lesster laughed. "In Africa, there's a saying that goes: *You have a watch, but we have the time.*

"The pace of life here is very, very slow. When I first came here for a cup of coffee, I waited for 45 minutes before the waitress appeared with a can of instant coffee powder, a cup of hot water and sugar!

"This was one of the greatest challenges I faced when I first arrived. Coming from Singapore where everything is done chop-chop, I had to get used to a different pace of life altogether. Sometimes I have to wait for two to three hours for a farmer. They are not lazy, they are just laidback. There is no concept of time and planning."

"Wasn't that hard for you to adjust to?" I asked curiously.

"Very hard," Lesster admitted.

He revealed that when he had left Singapore, he had not just been seeking a mid-life change, he had also been running away from the bitterness of a divorce.

"I used to be an egotistical, arrogant man who spent my life chasing after the 5C's," admitted Lesster. "Despite my success, my life was one big mess with no direction. I was chasing material wealth that turned out to be an illusion of happiness. In chasing after the 5C's, I had neglected a big portion of my life — relationships. After my divorce I felt ashamed and didn't dare face my mum and siblings. I felt like the black sheep of the family. I left for Uganda on Valentine's Day in 2001. By running away I was trying to erase my past."

The turning point for Lesster came in the unlikely form of beekeeping.

Handling bees slowly taught him the meaning of a relationship — learning to understand and respect other points of view. In falling in love with his craft and with his bees, he had acquired an attitude of patience, tolerance and co-existence with others. His bees taught him how to *zuo ren*, be a better person.

When he revealed all this with the cameras rolling, he made a big impact on my camera crew and me. We had not expected this level of frankness. It took a lot of courage to be so open. But I could see that Lesster had had the humility to transform himself into a kinder, gentler, wiser soul. I wondered what his family in Singapore would think as they watched him on television.

> *Who would have thought that Nature, and something as small as a bee, can transform a man with a hardened heart?*

Who would have thought that Nature, and something as small as a bee, can transform a man with a hardened heart?

In Nature he had released his ego and found humility and self worth.

One of his closest friends in Uganda, businessman Sekeran Vellasamy, described a perceptible change in Lesster over the years, "He has become a giver."

Lesster's generosity is seen in his involvement with a local school, where he helps to provide additional income by commissioning the school pottery teacher to make the little clay huts for the packaging of his honey. He also helps to stock the library with boxes of books donated by friends in Singapore.

"A lot of the children here had never even seen books before. It was a window to the world for these children," Lesster said.

Before I left Uganda, Lesster took me to the verdant foothills of Queen Elizabeth Park where he produced a small plant.

Children at the local school which Lesster supports financially and with donated books sent from well-wishers in Singapore.

The little coffee shoot which I planted on the slopes overlooking Queen Elizabeth National Park before I left Uganda. I wonder how tall it has grown!

"In Uganda we have a tradition," he said, handing me the plant, roots and all. "We get visitors to plant a tree to signify new life. This is a coffee plant."

Helping me to *changkol* the soil and plant my tree, he said, "Now you've given new life to this land."

***

Seven years later...

Lesster is back in Singapore for his annual trip home. Having lived in Africa for the past 14 years, he still comes back every year to eat his fill of chicken rice, *meepok tah*, curry chicken and *yong taufu*.

He has moved to Rwanda and is working with the Singapore Business Federation to set up the beekeeping industry there. But "my roots are still in Singapore, no doubt about it".

It always makes me happy to see Lesster, not only because he brings jars of his wonderful honey for me, but also because I am glad to see how he has made peace with his life and his relationships.

Everyone deals with setbacks in life. Sometimes a divorce, a personal failure or bankruptcy can seem like a crisis we cannot recover from. Lesster showed me that it is important not to give up but to be an overcomer in the face of setbacks. Through humility, open-mindedness and determination, he turned his crisis into an opportunity.

So the Little Honey Man turned out to be one of my greatest inspirations in life.

> ❝ *Lesster showed me that it is important not to give up but to be an overcomer in the face of setbacks. Through humility, open-mindedness and determination, he turned his crisis into an opportunity.* ❞

The beautifully rustic Compass Lodge before the 2014 fire (top), and after the devastating inferno that razed the lodge to the ground (bottom).

shangri-la

JOE & CAROL: MAKING DREAMS FROM DUST

The fire was devastating.

Fierce flames leapt several storeys into the air as the relentless inferno consumed not just buildings, businesses and homes, but also life savings, family mementoes and dreams.

Joseph Keh and his wife Caroline Lalmalsawmi, who had spent 10 years imagining into reality a traveller's lodge in the Old Town of Shangri-la, China, stood with their local staff and wept as together they watched their dreams turn to ashes.

The day after the fire, I received a text from Joe:

Hi… Shangri-la Old Town had a big fire… Compass is burnt to the ground. Please remember us.

The briefness of the text contrasted with the emotional turmoil I knew Joe had to be feeling. I was shocked to the core.

At that point it had been six years since 2008 when we had filmed Joe and Carol for the second season of *Find Me a Singaporean*. But I remembered how touched I had been by their warm hospitality when I visited Shangri-la, the fabled land of the classic novel and movie *Lost Horizon*.

✷✷✷

The very name of Shangri-la conjures up images of a secret paradise that only a privileged few discover.

For this city girl living in Singapore, where everything is within a 45-minute drive max, I found the journey to mystical Shangri-la appropriately arduous.

My cameraman, producer and I had flown from Singapore to Kunming, then to Lijiang — a journey of about 2,955km — from which we were to catch another flight to Shangri-la.

But at the Lijiang airport we were told, "*Dui bu chi,* sorry, foreigners are not allowed to fly to Shangri-la today because of political unrest."

Our bags were packed, production had begun, our team was all prepared to film in Shangri-la… and we were stuck in Lijiang, 175km short of our destination.

By hook or by crook, we had to find our way there.

The good news was that it was still possible to get to Shangri-la. We would just have to take the more traditional route — by road. The driver of the red taxi that we clambered into predicted a four-hour drive on the windy mountain road.

From time to time the driver would reassure us, "Just ahead. Almost there." After a three-hour nap, we woke up to the familiar refrain, "Just ahead. Almost there."

Shangri-la sits at an elevation of 3,280m above sea level. The effects of the increasing altitude and thinning air as we drove on hour after hour, up and up, began to take its toll on my producer and cameraman, both of whom were feeling a little nauseous.

Surprisingly I felt fine. I had heard that short people sometimes escape the effects of altitude sickness. If that were the case, this was one time I was happy to be short!

The mythical and remote Shangri-la, previously known as Zhongdian, is located in the far north where Tibet, Sichuan and Yunnan converge.

The cobblestone streets of Shangri-la Old Town are flanked by traditional Tibetan tea houses, shops and guesthouses.

Finally after seven long hours — hadn't the driver said *four?* — we saw a sign proclaiming: *SHANGRI-LA*. We were here!

***

It is said that in ancient times, Shangri-la — or Zhongdian as it was previously known — together with Litang in Sichuan and Batang in Tibet combined to create the fiefdom of the three sons of a Tibetan king. Zhongdian was officially renamed Shangri-la, Tibetan for *Sun and Moon in Heart,* in 2001.

Natural attractions with mythical names like Stone Forest, Tiger Leaping Gorge and Jade Dragon Snow Mountain draw tourists from all over the world.

The fascinating blend of Tibetan and Han Chinese architecture, food and costumes is a result of Shangri-la county being located in the far north of Yunnan, where Tibet, Sichuan and Yunnan converge.

As with many Chinese townships, Shangri-la's modern section bristles with contemporary apartments and shops. But it is the old quarter, also known as *Gu Zheng* or Ancient Town, that is the soul of the capital. *Gu Zheng* is believed to have been built 1,300 years ago and was an important landmark along the Silk Route.

It was in this ancient quarter of Shangri-la that I was to find our Singaporean, Joe.

***

There is a captivating blend of Tibetan and Han Chinese culture in Shangri-la, evident in its architecture, food and costumes.

Wandering along the narrow cobblestone streets, I passed rows of traditional Tibetan teahouses, shops and guesthouses with wooden screens exquisitely carved with auspicious symbols. Strings of red lanterns hanging from the roofs swayed to and fro, lending an air of stateliness to the scene.

Men and women in richly-coloured, long-sleeved shirts, padded vests, long skirts and oversized hats tied under the chin with strips of cotton walked briskly by with woven baskets on their back.

At the town square, cloth buntings of prayer flags in yellow, pink, blue and red fluttered in the wind, while women with weather-beaten faces beckoned from street stalls selling ethnic jewellery, fabric and dried herbs.

Everywhere I looked, the bright colours reflected the vibrancy of this centuries-old town. I felt like I was on a movie set of ancient China.

My reverie was broken by a wiry man on a three-wheeled bicycle pulling a cart. Rolling to a stop a stone's throw from me, he called out in Mandarin, "Are you Belinda?"

"Yes, are you Joe?" I said expectantly.

"No, no I'm one of Joe's staff. I was sent to meet you. Here, put your luggage in my cart and I will show you the way."

Heaving my bag into the cart, the man peddled away so quickly that I was left running after him, yelling, "Not so fast, *si fu*! *Si fu*! Not so fast!"

Just when I started to panic, thinking that my luggage had been bag-napped, another man stepped into my path.

"Hi Belinda, welcome! I'm Joe!" said the tanned man with closely cropped hair.

Are you really a Singaporean? I ask Joe when I come face to face with this weatherbeaten man who looks more like a park ranger than a city boy!

My first reaction was, "Are you really a Singaporean?"

With his lean, weathered face, North Face jacket and woollen hat, he looked more like an outdoor guide or park ranger than someone who had grown up in urban Singapore.

He burst out laughing. "Yes, I am!"

I immediately took a liking to this man's lack of airs. Leading the way to his four-year-old lodge The Compass, Joe, then 38, introduced me to Carol, his pretty wife with the chocolate eyes, and they related the story of how they had ended up in Shangri-la, far away from Singapore and their relatives.

***

Joe met his wife, whom he jokingly called his "rib", while he was serving in a non-government organisation in Shillong, northeast India. At that time, Carol was doing her Master's degree at the local university and the two recognised in each other a common love for adventure.

It was during their honeymoon that they first encountered Shangri-la while backpacking through Yunnan and were so taken by its charm that they decided to build a lodge-cum-café for tourists in the ancient town.

"Four years ago when I saw this place, it was a pig sty," said Joe wryly. Opening his laptop, he showed me photos of the derelict state of the original building, rubble piled high everywhere. When he signed a 15-year contract to rebuild the place, people had called him mad.

The Compass Lodge and Café is a thoughtfully appointed home away from home for many a traveller to Shangri-la.

The stunning beauty of the countryside has given rise to natural attractions with mythical names like Jade Dragon Snow Mountain and Tiger Leaping Gorge.

"'Why on earth would you want to live in a place like this?' That was the general reaction," said Joe with a chuckle. "But I saw the potential here. I visualised a comfortable place where people could rest. A place of peace."

Established in 2004, the lodge, with its rustic wood panelling and natural stone features, became a home away from home for many a traveler from Asia, Europe, the US and China who had come to Shangri-la for trekking, photography and sightseeing holidays.

Golden sunlight streamed in through large picture windows and inviting sofas with plump cushions and Chinese throw rugs added cosy accents. An extensive café menu offered comfort food including burgers, pizzas, kebabs, stews, milkshakes and lemon pound cake. Pastries beckoned from beneath glass domes glistening on the café counter.

***

But it did not take long for me to realise that The Compass was far more than a place of wood and stone. It was a place where dreams were springing to life.

The rural villagers whom Joe and Carol hired to work at The Compass came looking for a job, a place to sleep, a meal to fill their stomach — nothing more. A hard life had drummed into them the futility of lofty aspirations.

Then they saw Joe and Carol's vision taking shape in front of their astonished eyes.

Without experience in either construction or hospitality, the couple designed and supervised the development of every detail of The Compass, from the café to the guestrooms to the kitchen, including thoughtful details like books in the café for browsing and hand-made quilts on the four-poster guest beds.

To the villagers who were used to everything staying the same for 10, 15, 50 years in Shangri-la, Joe and Carol appeared to be creating something from nothing, making possible the impossible.

"When I first came here everything looked very rundown," recalled Lily, who was one of the first local kitchen staff to be hired. "Honestly, I never thought it would become the place it is today. That was the first time I had ever seen a dream come alive! It made me realise that if you follow the dream in your heart, you can do a lot of big things."

> *It made me realise that if you follow the dream in your heart, you can do a lot of big things.*

Increasingly Joe and Carol were drawn into the lives of their resilient and assiduous staff, who averaged just 19 years of age.

"Before I came here, I didn't know anything," said Azom, a kitchen hand deft at making dumplings. "But Joe and Carol trained me to be the best worker I can be. My dream is to become as good a chef as Tom (the American head chef)."

Lily added, "The overall feeling here is that everyone is family. That's the reason I am here."

Joe and Carol threw a welcome dinner for our camera crew that evening, inviting all the staff. We made a cheerful party of about 15 people, sitting at two tables laden with small dishes of meat, vegetables and condiments surrounding tin steamboats with extra tall chimneys. A fragrant steam was rising from the bubbling broth.

"Welcome to Shangri-la," toasted Joe with a glass of yak butter tea as the staff clapped.

I remember it was so cold that we all kept our sweaters and woollies on during dinner. Yet as we chatted, joked, laughed and ate together, there was a palpable warmth in the room of the kind that is only found when people are in the company of loved ones.

***

Early the next morning, we set off in Joe's four-wheel drive for the remote mountain village of one of his young workers, Zhu Ma. This round-eyed, apple-cheeked 19 year old was the sole breadwinner of her family.

Joe drove long distances to personally take his workers back to their villages for home visits. Today's journey would take us almost six hours one way.

As we drove into the mountains surrounding Shangri-la, the sun was just breaking and I could see why this place had taken on a storied aura.

Checkered rice fields fanned out from farms. Shaggy-backed yaks with graceful horns grazed in flat grasslands that rolled away as far as eye could see.

As we left the town and travelled deeper into the wilderness, mysterious lakes glistened in the shadow of spectacular mountains that marched one after another into the horizon, the farthest peaks appearing to float in the morning mist.

Further yet, the paved pass became a dirt road, causing Joe's car to bounce along the winding route. To our right, a rocky slope fell away into a rushing river fed by melting glacial snow.

Occasionally we would pass villagers on foot, bent from rattan baskets filled with firewood on their back.

I fell asleep at some point, but Zhu Ma was way too excited to feel sleepy. It had been a year since she had seen her ageing parents.

As the sun crossed over to the other side of the sky, we finally drove into a tiny hamlet of stone and wood homes. Mounds of dried hay leaned against farmhouses.

Carol, whom Joe jokingly calls his "rib", greets me with characteristic warmth. Zhu Ma (top right) joins us on a visit to a local home where we gather around the crackling hearth to drink yak butter tea (bottom).

Finally, the end of our journey! I thought.

But I was mistaken. This was just as far as the car could go. The rest of the journey to Zhu Ma's home would have to be on foot.

Behind the hamlet, a mountain trail wound upwards towards a few houses roosting on the steep slopes, more than an hour's hike away. One of them was Zhu Ma's.

Loose pebbles made the path treacherous and landslides had crumbled part of the trail. But I was determined to make it up the mountain as I was carrying some precious cargo for Zhu Ma's father — a pair of metal crutches bought with Zhu Ma's hard earned money

We had ascended so high that the farmhouses in the hamlet looked like tiny dolls' houses nestled in the valley, the river a green ribbon winding its way into the distance. Towards the horizon, the higher mountains were frosted with snow.

But after almost two hours of the uphill climb, I was too tired to appreciate the view. I was still recovering from a bout of dengue fever and it was all I could do to shuffle my way up, stopping every now and then with my hands on my knees to catch my breath. I confess the crutches came in handy… I leant on them a few times and at other times Joe used the crutch to pull me up the slope. Truly pathetic!

Villagers navigated this path every day. But the ageing, like Zhu Ma's parents, found it increasingly difficult.

Just when my legs were turning to *tofu*, Joe pointed up ahead and said cheerfully, "Look Belinda! *Dao le*, we're here. You can see Zhu Ma's house, only 15 minutes away! *Jiayou, jiayou!*"

I believe I was too spent to do anything but grunt.

Exhausted as we were, there was excitement in the air at the prospect of meeting Zhu Ma's family and seeing her father's reaction to his daughter's thoughtful gift.

When we made it to Zhu Ma's squat, stone house, we found a petite, bespectacled man in an army cap sitting on a roughly hewn wooden bench outside.

Zhu Ma beamed at the sight of her father. There were no emotional scenes — that was not their way. Wordlessly, but with pride shining in her eyes, Zhu Ma handed the crutches to her father, who accepted them with interest.

"*Shu Shu!* Uncle!" Joe called out. "*Ni hao!* This is my Singapore friend, Belinda!"

"*Ni hao, ni hao,*" greeted *Shu Shu* with a broad smile.

"I am sorry it is so difficult to get up here," he apologised.

I straightened my back. "Difficult? No, no. Not one bit," I said, ignoring my creaking knees.

Shu Shu had a left foot that was turned inwards and wasting away due to disease. Zhu Ma helped her father stand as Joe adjusted and readjusted the height of the crutches.

Zhu Ma's mother, dressed in layers against the mountain chill and sporting a bright blue cap, emerged from the house at the sound of her daughter's voice.

"*Ah Yi*, Zhu Ma is very happy today because she has brought her *Baba* a gift!" Joe said, pointing to Zhu Ma's father, who was still sitting at his bench with one crutch in his hands. Turning it all around, he was examining it closely… now holding it like a rifle and peering down its length, now bringing it close to study the screws.

"*Wah!*" he was saying with barely contained excitement. "*Wah!*"

He was like a small boy fiddling with a new toy. The look of pure pleasure on his face touched me. For the last 40 years he had been using a tree branch as his walking stick.

Shu Shu used his new crutches to hobble into his house, down two steps into a dim and cluttered room with a dirt floor. Zhu Ma, the teenaged breadwinner of the family, was trying to make enough money to build her parents a second storey so that they did not have to sleep on the ground floor with their livestock.

"I really respect Zhu Ma," Joe said when we were sitting outside the home, taking in the fresh mountain air. "For such a young girl to leave her family to go out to work… I don't know how she does it. I've learnt a lot from her.

"Money is important to her but she doesn't work just for the money. It's because she wants to learn some skills and she has a lot of determination.

Top: Trekking up the mountain to Zhu Ma's remote home. Bottom left: The young girl presents a gift of lightweight crutches to her father, who has been using a tree branch for 40 years.

Whatever we do to help, I want her to know that she's a part of this whole process. It's not just my doing.

"Carol and I are just a springboard for our team members. In the end, they need to learn to tackle life's challenges on their own."

Joe's sense of responsibility to his staff was genuine and heartfelt.

"When Zhu Ma first came to me, I asked her what her dream was. She replied, 'Brother Joe, I take one day at a time. Today if I have rice to eat and a place to lay my head, that is enough.' But I told her, 'That is not enough. What happens when Joe and Carol are no longer around? What will you do then?' So I encourage my team members to think ahead, to plan, to have ambitions and goals.

"Carol and I have learnt that when you set your mind on something, you cannot give up. The Compass is like a marathon for Zhu Ma, Azom, and all the other staff. Carol and I can only run alongside them, helping where we can and encouraging them. When I see how hard they fight to succeed, I know that we cannot give up even when the going gets tough. They have become like our little sisters and brothers."

Looking at the plucky teenager as she squatted in front of her seated mother and lay her hands on her mother's lap, gazing intently into the eyes she had missed for a year, I could see why Joe felt compelled to help her and her family.

Before we left, Zhu Ma had another gift — this one was for her mother.

"I would like to sing a song of blessing to *Mama*," she said shyly. She sang then, her voice sweet and guileless. The chorus of *"Mama, I bless you, I bless you"* brought tears to her eyes and she choked up.

It must have been overwhelming for such a young girl to strike out alone in a strange town, shouldering the full responsibility of looking after her family.

"Don't be sad, don't be sad," soothed Joe, patting the young girl on the shoulder. "You are doing well. You have made your *Mama* and *Baba* very happy."

By the time we left Zhu Ma's home to make our journey back to The Compass, the sun was setting. We faced the prospect of a long drive back to Shangri-la in pitch darkness as there were no street lamps in the mountains.

I was bone tired. But I would not have traded that day for anything in the world.

I had seen the rewards of selflessness that day — rewards that were intangible, but immeasurable.

***

Characteristic of their kindness, Joe and Carol also fostered a five-year-old boy, Dorje, the nephew of one of their staff.

The bright eyed, cherry-cheeked little tyke had an infectious grin and wore his trademark striped beanie pulled low over his eyebrows, bright eyes peeking out from under the brim.

Dorje had been abandoned by his parents — a situation not uncommon in Shangri-la, according to Joe. The Singaporean couple took Dorje in and sent him to school. On weekends they drove him back to his village to visit his grandparents.

That weekend I tagged along on one of Dorje's visits. The land was dry and flat in his village. A few black cows with wicked looking horns trotted about freely.

Typically, the ground level of local houses is for livestock, with the family living on the second level accessible by a ladder or rudimentary wooden steps.

Dorje was so little that he had to clamber up the steps with both hands and feet.

"*Nai Nai!*" Dorje's childish voice rang out as he ran to his grandmother, who hugged her grandson and held his face with both hands, looking for any changes since she last saw him.

Dorje's *Nai Nai* wore the many-layered garb of the Tibetans. An embroidered vest and a red, woollen cap added cheerful accents to her worn dress. From under her cap, two girlish braids hung down her back, making a charming contrast to her wrinkled face.

Dorje clearly adored his *Ye Ye*, a farmer with a lined face under an old fur hat. Reaching up, the little tyke put one arm around his *Ye Ye*'s shoulders and grinned at him. Dorje's twinkling eyes were a reflection of his grandfather's.

We sat on low stools outside the home.

"We know that Dorje is very happy as he grows up in your care," said *Nai Nai* to Joe and Carol. "Even though we don't get to see him all the time, our hearts are at ease."

"Don't mention it, don't mention it," replied Joe, embarrassed at the gratitude. "Dorje is really adorable. He is a cute and smart child and there is no reason he should not be getting an education. Carol and I want to be alongside him as he grows up. It's our privilege."

There is another positive outcome of their involvement with Dorje, Zhu Ma and the other citizens of the Shangri-la community.

"When we get involved in the welfare of the local families, our team can see that we are not just here to run a business but that we care for them like our own family. We are all in this journey together," Joe told me.

The irrepressible Dorje, a young child fostered by Joe and Carol, at his grandparents' traditional home, where drying animal parts hang from the ceiling like so much ham.

Six years later…

In disbelief I read news article after news article about the 10-hour inferno that had swept through Shangri-la Old Town in the early hours of January 11th, 2014. The blaze, which was rumoured to have been sparked by outdated and faulty electrical wiring in one of the old buildings, spread quickly.

Unable to get fire engines through the narrow alleyways of the 1,300-year-old town, thousands of firefighters and law enforcement officers could only watch helplessly as almost 250 ancient buildings were razed to the ground and a further 43 were demolished to prevent the fire from spreading. The only consolation was that, miraculously, there had been no casualties.

One of the buildings that was destroyed was Joe and Carol's beautiful lodge.

At the time of the fire, The Compass was actually closed for the winter, and the couple was in Kunming together with their staff for a three-day company retreat.

"It was the last night of the retreat and we were headed to Thailand the next morning," recalled Joe. "But instead we received a call from a friend in Shangri-la saying, 'There is a huge fire. I don't think The Compass is going to survive.'

"We couldn't believe it. Forfeiting our tickets to Thailand, we returned to Shangri-la the next day on the first available flight."

The sight that met their eyes was shocking.

"There was dirt, glass shards and embers everywhere. The whole Old Town was enveloped in thick smoke and the military had completely shut the Old Town down," recalled Joe. "We could barely get back to the site.

"Everything at The Compass had burnt down. The only thing that was left was our old fireplace, which was standing strong in the midst of the rubble and the devastation all around. We just broke down and cried.

"It was not just because of the building but the memories and the years of hard work that we were mourning."

Their staff was equally devastated. Huddling closely, they wept together. Four of the staff had lost all their worldly possessions.

"That night we all camped in our house, eating instant noodles and braving the winter's night. Ironically it snowed the next morning and for the following few days."

The inferno which swept through Shangri-la Old Town in 2014 is reported to have destroyed 250 ancient buildings.

Devastated staff of The Compass stand among the rubble — four of them had lost all their worldly possessions. Everything was razed to the ground except an old fireplace (bottom).

***

But the tragedy was not the end for The Compass.

"The fire only made us more resilient," said Joe resolutely. "Ironically, it gave us international publicity and more people came to know about us than before!"

Their fortitude kicked in and they found themselves planning harder, working faster, dreaming bigger.

Joe and Carol could have packed up, closed that chapter of their lives and gone home to Singapore. But they could not find it in their heart to give up.

"Many things went through our mind, but the thought of leaving was not one of them," said Joe. "Instead we concentrated on our next step — how to press on. Mainly for our local staff who had become our family."

They knew they had to rebuild what they had nurtured for the last 10 years. The encouragement and donations that came pouring in from friends and even strangers all over the world — Singapore, Taiwan, US, Europe, and within China — were just the impetus they needed to rebuild.

But the biggest, and most moving, surprise for the couple was how the entire Compass family rallied together.

"One of our local staff had been saving money to build a house for his widowed mother in Dali. But he knew that financially it was tough for us. Without any hesitation he withdrew the money from his bank and handed it to us. We did not ask for it. That was all he had left and he gave it to us," Joe said with emotion.

"Another staff from the Tibetan village donated her laptop that her father had given her and emptied her bank account of RMB 1,500 (about S$330)."

On their own volition, all the staff decided not to accept salaries until The Compass was back on its feet. For two months they went without a salary even to the point of personal financial distress.

"One staff member nearly couldn't come back to work for us this year because her family felt that she earned too little and forbade her from returning to us," said Joe. "But she did!"

Joe and Carol had seen them through tough times and now they were determined to see Joe and Carol through uncertainties.

Astonishingly, with everyone's contributions and efforts big and small, The Compass was rebuilt within three months.

Everyone was emotional at seeing The Compass relaunched on June 8th, 2014. They were one of the few businesses that had kept their entire team after the fire.

From a skeletal staff of five to six at the start, The Compass today has grown to a staff strength of 28. The local team works in the kitchen, the café and a new enterprise on the premises: a farm.

"We realised that not all the staff are suited for hospitality work and so we developed a farm specially for a group of handicapped and socially challenged staff," Joe explained.

"Ironically, after the fire our staff numbers grew noticeably… to the point of an 'explosion' of people wanting to join us!"

On Mondays The Compass is closed so that the entire team has a chance to "rest and fellowship over a hearty potluck dinner that bonds us together as a family".

In 2009 one more person joined the Compass family: Hope Lalremruati Keh, Joe and Carol's daughter. Born in Singapore, Hope returned with her parents to Shangri-la when she was just three months old.

Now aged six, Hope goes to kindergarten in Shangri-la, speaks the local dialect and drinks yak butter tea.

"There is no mall, no children's playground and no kids' activities in Shangri-la, so she really looks forward to visiting Singapore — even going to NTUC supermarket gives her a thrill!" said Joe, laughing. "But living in Shangri-la, she is widely exposed to different cultures and personality types."

Far from interrupting their life in Shangri-la, young Hope "came into this environment complementing us and bringing much joy to the whole team", said Joe with paternal pride.

Little Dorje is now in Primary 5. He has been growing well and the Kehs have returned him to his adoring grandparents.

Four more children, with backgrounds similar to Dorje's, have been taken in by Joe and Carol. Currently two girls, aged seven and 10, are still living with them.

If I had admired Joe and Carol before, I admire them even more now.

With the support of well wishers and the loyal staff, who rallied round Joe and Carol, the new Compass rose from the ashes within three months! Bottom right: Joe and Carol celebrate Singapore's 50th birthday in Shangri-la.

How many people can emerge from a tragedy stronger than before? They had not suffered a small setback — they had lost *everything* overnight.

"It's not important how we start but how we persevere and pick ourselves up so that we finish the race of our lives," said Joe simply.

"Our vision is to empower our local staff to reach their highest potential and to impart to them planning and management skills so that they can one day stand on their own two feet and even help their own people."

Hope Lalremruati Keh, Joe and Carol's daughter, was born in Singapore and now lives with her parents in Shangri-la, where she speaks the local dialect and drinks yak butter tea.

> *It's not important how we start but how we persevere and pick ourselves up so that we finish the race of our lives.*

I believe Joe and Carol could not have rebuilt The Compass so quickly if they had not seen the fruit of the seeds they had sown in the lives of the local people for the past 11 years.

They were not fulfilling a dream for two. They were fulfilling a dream for the entire Compass family.

Said Joe, "We realise that when you are faithful in following through your vision, you grow in unexpected ways, and that is when your dream becomes bigger than you!"

The Compass family posing for a rare photo taken on a chilly autumn day in 2015.

> *When you are faithful in following through your vision, you grow in unexpected ways, and that is when your dream becomes bigger than you!*

The homeless in Mongolia's capital, Ulaanbaatar, brave sub zero temperatures on a daily basis. Some live in manholes meant for maintaining gas pipes.

mongolia

DAVID: FEEDING THE HUNGRY

The corpulent winter clouds were heavy with snow, casting a grey pall over the street. It was an ordinary street, with wooden electricity poles on the sidewalks and vehicles rumbling over circular iron manholes.

Then one of the manholes gave a lurch.

Gratingly it shifted a few inches to the side, and out of the ground emerged a man's head.

"Hello," I said uncertainly to the man as he emerged a little more so that a worn cap and disheveled clothes were apparent.

Squatting down to be closer to eye level with him, I said, "You live here?"

"Yes," he said in Mongolian. "I live under the street where the gas pipes are."

Hesitantly I peeked into the dark hole. The space was the size of the inside of a car, with a short ladder leading down from the street. In the blackness I could just make out two other men lying on their side in the dirt, oblivious to the cockroaches skittering from crack to crevice. Their pillows were plastic bags stuffed with the scraps of their existence.

Getting ready to film a picnic in the freezing cold!

"There used to be five of us living here, but now there are three," said the man. Even three men living cheek by jowl would make for a cramped fit. I struggled to imagine how five could manage. The man answered my upspoken question.

"When there are five of us, we have no room to move. We sit in one position hugging our knees. We have to be very careful not to touch the gas pipes. One man died touching the gas pipe."

The man had no family and no friends. Jobless and homeless, this underground cavity had been his sanctuary for the past three years.

"I don't like sleeping here," he said wistfully. "It's not a home and you have no peace."

As he spoke, the snow started to fall. He was anxious to return to the meagre warmth underground. I shook his hand and the last I saw of him was the top of his cap sliding into the subterranean cavern and disappearing from sight.

***

My camera crew and I had landed in 1,351m high Ulaanbaatar, the capital of Mongolia, in winter — which was not surprising, considering winter stayed put seven months out of a year. January and February temperatures of -20°C are common for most of Mongolia, plunging to -40°C on winter nights.

Much of the ground is covered with permafrost for part of the year, making farming, livestock herding, construction, mining and road building a challenge.

Much of the ground in Mongolia is covered with permafrost for part of the year, making farming, livestock herding, construction and mining a challenge.

A vast country of over 1.5 million sq km, Mongolia is the world's second largest land-locked country, and also one of the most sparsely populated with an estimated population of only 3 million people. More than 30% of them live in Ulaanbaatar.

We were here to film retired Singaporean engineer, David Szeto, 60. David hated cold weather and he hated mutton — both of which were in plentiful supply in Mongolia. Some would have said he was in the wrong place. But, to David, there was nowhere else he wanted to be.

A vast land of over 1.5 million sq km, Mongolia is the world's second largest land-locked country and also one of the most sparsely populated.

As a director at Lamp of the Path, the humanitarian arm of Buddhist foundation FPMT Mongolia, David oversaw the running of a soup kitchen, a health clinic and a child development programme.

Bespectacled and avuncular, David met us at the airport together with his Mongolian secretary Jaagii.

"Hey, Belinda!" he smiled amiably, turning to introduce Jaagii.

"David! I'm so happy to meet you!" I replied.

As we drove through the city streets to Lamp of the Path, Ulaanbaatar looked like any Asian city to me, with bumper to bumper traffic, modern high rises and hoardes of milling pedestrians.

In this fabled land of Genghis Khan, his legacy is everywhere, from the name of the Chinggis Khan International Airport to the 40m high statue of Genghis majestically astride a horse along the Tuul River, where he is said to have discovered a golden whip. The Mongol Empire, founded by Genghis, had once upon a time stretched from Ukraine in the west to Korea in the east, from Siberia in the north to the Gulf of Oman and Vietnam in the south, with a thriving nomadic people that numbered a quarter of the earth's total population.

Ulaanbaatar is home to ornate religious temples and artistic tributes to the fabled Genghis Khan.

But during my visit in 2012, this magnificent land characterised by grassy steppe, mountains and the Gobi desert, had more than the harsh weather to grapple with. Unemployment, alcoholism and homelessness among its people were causing social and economic strain.

World Bank statistics show that more than a quarter of Mongolians live below the poverty line, existing on less than S$1.70 a day. Up to 60% of Ulaanbaatar's 1.1 million people live in slums.

As we left the city and made our way to the soup kitchen in the poorest part of the district, tall buildings gave way to bleak barrenness. The landscape was an overwhelming brown at that time of the year — brown earth, leaning brown electricity poles, wooden brown shacks with zinc roofs that looked like they might blow away in the wind, broken-down brown fences under a cold, cloudless sky. And in the distance the mountains, always the mountains.

People on the street wore multiple layers of pants, vests, jackets and headwear against the cold. Children played football on the hard-packed earth. Others as young as seven or eight walked hand in hand with even younger siblings.

***

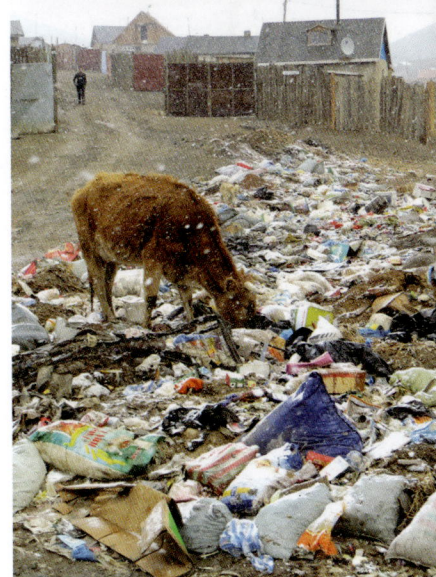

Lamp of the Path's soup kitchen operates from one of the poorest parts of the city.

Lamp of the Path's soup kitchen, located in a low brick building, opened its doors daily at 1.30pm. But long before then, a line of people would form at its door.

They were of all ages and sizes: bent women in thick coats, wrinkled men with walking sticks, ruddy-cheeked babies bouncing on the hip of young mothers with hoods drawn over their forehead. The old ones waited in the bitter cold in long-suffering silence. The children laughingly played games and bantered with each other. Some were homeless, some came from the surrounding slums. Many of them had walked a long way for their only hot meal of the day.

"It's really, really cold. What do you think the temperature is right now?" I asked David, as I blew on my gloved hands trying to warm some life into them.

"About 5°C to 10°C below freezing," replied David.

The penetrating cold was mind numbing. I was wearing padded winter clothes, yet standing outside the soup kitchen for barely 10 minutes had reduced me to stutters.

Every day David would mingle with the 80 or so homeless people queueing at lunchtime.

"Just imagine you don't have dinner one night and you go hungry through the whole morning, how do you feel?" he said. "I cannot say I know what it is like to suffer like they suffer."

Scores of people walk a long way for their only hot meal of the day at Lamp of the Path.

Lamp of the Path runs a soup kitchen and medical centre for the destitute, as well as a school for children.

As we spoke, the snow started to fall. Concerned, David opened the doors early. After the cutting cold outside, stepping into the warmth of the dining room was like stepping into a warm embrace.

The centre also distributed donated clothes, and there would be an air of excitement as each person stepped up to select one piece of clothing. *Should I choose the warmest or should I choose the prettiest?* You could see the conflict in their eyes. Eventually, oversized and undersized clothing — they were all gratefully taken. These would be worn continuously until they gave out.

Snow begins to fall as we make our way to Duurengaral's house in a nearby slum.

Nutritious meals are prepared in an orderly, spotless kitchen.

In the kitchen, the cook Yili and an assistant had been busy since early morning, frying flatbreads, stirring stews and warming salted milk tea in deep pots. The kitchen was spotless and organised, and in their chef whites and neat aprons, the two looked like they were running a professional kitchen.

On long wooden tables, they set soft buns next to cheerful blue bowls of thick, steaming stew, chockfull of carrots, potatoes, pasta and shreds of meat. Resources were limited, said David, and this was the best they could offer.

There was a genial hubbub as frozen hands and feet slowly thawed in the plain but cosy dining room and the simple meal was eaten among familiar faces not related by blood but connected by circumstance.

As bread was dipped in stew and salted milk tea was drunk from bowls, a nurse in a scrub cap and face mask circulated, chatting and taking notes on those who needed medical care.

In the white-tiled medical room off the dining area, a man was waiting for consultation. He only ate once each day, he told us, and walked for an hour to the soup kitchen for his daily meal. He had high blood pressure. Lately his vision had blurred inexplicably and his breathing was laboured, making it difficult for him to walk long distances.

Another woman was having her head bandaged.

"*Sain-baina-uu,* hello," I greeted her. She may have been in her thirties or forties, but looked older, with the wind-toughened face of someone who spent a great deal of time out in the harsh elements.

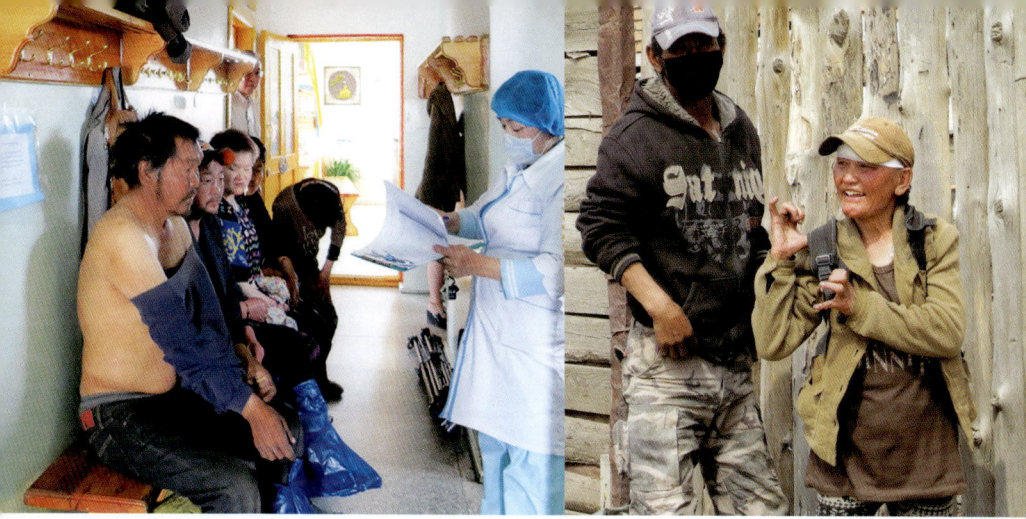

After lunch, a nurse attends to those who need medical attention, including this tough woman (right, in brown) who was beaten up on the streets where she lives.

Every day she came to have her head wound cleaned and a new bandage applied. She was homeless and had been set upon by strangers on the street, leaving her with a bleeding gash on her head. For the last seven or eight years she had lived alone near the river not far away, she told us, but it took her three hours to get to the centre for lunch because she stopped to pick rubbish along the way. A bag of recyclable bits could earn her 2 cents.

"You must protect your head," I said to her with concern through an interpreter. To my surprise, this tough-looking woman broke down. Perhaps it had been a long time since anyone had offered her a kind word.

"I am just an ordinary woman and I can't protect myself," she said quietly.

Her tears stopped as abruptly as they had started. In her life, there was no room for self pity and as soon as her bandage was secured, she left. As she strode off in her man's pants and boots, a garbage bag half full of scavenged items slung over her shoulder and her bandaged head now hidden under a cap, she gave us a small smile and a wave. I have often wondered what has become of her.

***

Beyond the dining room were chipper green doors opening into sunlit classrooms where Lamp of the Path conducted its educational programme for about 70 children between the ages of three and 12.

The 16 Guidelines in Mongolia programme imparted to the children both basic academic knowledge and Buddhist values of living well, behaving well and filial piety.

Among these children were abandoned boys and girls, orphans, and those from poverty-stricken families, David said. Every single one wore neat clothes and had tidy hair — the centre emphasised self respect. Education was going to be their means of escaping an otherwise difficult life.

These kids came across as genuinely enjoying the camaraderie and the lessons in the classroom, even if some of them had to bring their baby brother or sister to school with them, jiggling the little one on their knee while lessons proceeded.

The wholehearted enthusiasm of the children was utterly endearing. I sat in the classroom watching a ponytailed preschooler with a freshly scrubbed face belting out a confident solo in front of her classmates, after which a group of young teens performed a K-pop inspired dance.

The wholehearted enthusiasm of the children is utterly endearing.

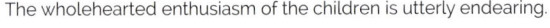

Although traditional Mongolian throat singing evokes the animal sounds of the wild and the echoes in the vast wilderness, these children provided a glimpse of a modern Mongolia that, for better or worse, was assimilating the pop cultures of the world.

***

Not all who needed medical help could make it to Lamp of the Path's medical centre. The next day David and I visited one of their house-bound beneficiaries.

Coming to school where they can eat, play and learn with friends is a highlight for many of the children, who hail from the nearby slums.

At the soup kitchen, David had shown me a photo of Duurengaral Togmid in her graduation gown at the age of 20, a rosy-cheeked girl with a level gaze, long dark hair and a penchant for pretty barrettes.

The next picture he showed me was of a pale, sick woman, over 150kg in weight, and bedridden in a stomach-down position because of severe pressure ulcers all over her buttocks and the back of both legs.

Uncomprehending, I asked David, "Who is this woman?" pointing to the second photo.

"That is what Duurengaral looks like now," he said to my shock. "Just after her graduation, she was found to have a pituitary tumour. Her father abandoned the family when she fell ill and she has been bedridden for seven years, with only her mother to take care of her."

Duurengaral was the only child in the family. She had done well at school and was at the cusp of a full life: a stable job, domestic comfort, romance. But just as she was within grasp of her dream life, it had turned into a mirage which crumbled into the reality of days, weeks and years of lying prone in a humble house with only her mother for company.

Duuregaral before she was stricken with debilitating illness.

No one visited, no one provided a distraction or held out hope. Her mother could not work or leave the house — caring for Duurengaral was a full-time job. Everything they had, even food, was a handout from charitable organisations like Lamp of the Path.

***

I had to psyche myself for two days before the visit to Duurengaral.

During that particular trip I was emotionally fragile, having just ended a six-year relationship that had almost led to marriage. It had not felt like a break-up, it had felt like a divorce. In front of the cameras I was chirpy and professional. Behind them I was a wreck, crying easily and losing so much weight that my producers were concerned. Meeting Duurengaral would be hard. I braced myself for a depressing hour and told myself that, whatever happened, I would not cry.

The house that Duurengaral shared with her mother was in a nearby shantytown. Once a week David took a volunteer doctor and his secretary-translator Jaagii with him on visits to shut-ins like Duurengaral.

Posters seeking support for Duurengaral are posted on public walls by Lamp of the Path.

David led our small procession down the mud trail, squeezing gamely through a hole in a fence to arrive at a tumble of shacks. Through another fence and there was Duurengaral's small house of brick and wood in the middle of a desolate brown yard where nothing grew.

Passing through a flimsy door, we entered the house — a room without cupboards but with all the memories and belongings of a mother and daughter neatly stacked up against the plaster walls: knick knacks and framed photographs from happier times, a small TV, religious objects.

Duurengaral's mother, a smiling woman wearing a black, cotton suit, greeted us warmly. My eye was drawn to a single bed against the wall where Duurengaral lay on her stomach.

She turned her face towards us and, unexpectedly, gave one of the most beatific smiles I had ever seen. Through her eyes gleamed an angelic purity that instantly touched me. She was wearing a plain t-shirt with a thin cotton blanket drawn up to her waist, but her hair was combed until it shined and her mother had wound the tresses into two Princess Leia buns above her ears where pretty earrings twinkled. On her finger was a bead ring made for her by her mother. The natural desire of this terminally ill girl to look pretty despite her circumstances was heartbreaking.

The rundown house where Duurengaral and her mother spend their days. Duurengaral's father abandoned the family when his daughter fell ill. Mother and daughter depend on the kindness of strangers for everything from food to medical care.

I had expected a depressed young woman, not this bright-eyed, smiling girl. I took her hand and she playfully arm wrestled me, laughing when she won easily.

"My power more than yours!" she said merrily.

The doctor raised the blanket to treat her pressure ulcers and the state of her buttocks and legs was like nothing I had ever seen. In her puffed up body, a dozen holes at least 3cm in diameter were bored deeply into her flesh. Her severe pressure ulcers had developed into open, sunken craters, damaging the tissue below. The more penetrating the pressure ulcers, the more likely the damage to muscle, bone, tendons and joints.

It was extremely difficult to watch the doctor remove the gauze from each wound and pull out intestine-long strips of cotton that had been inserted to absorb the pus. I winced each time and tried to distract Duurengaral with chatter. But the doctor told me that, in truth, Duurengaral could no longer feel any sensation any more. On top of her pituitary tumour and pressure ulcers, she also suffered from the effects of obesity, diabetes mellitus and

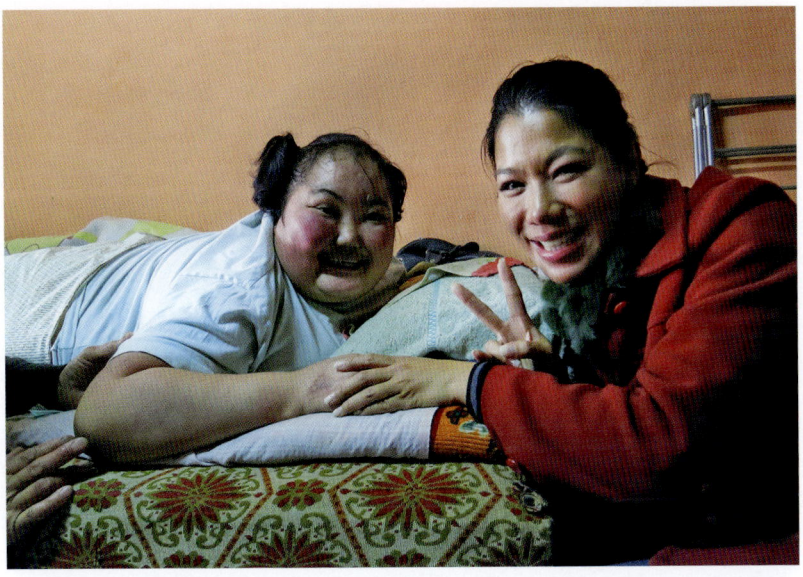

This photo of Duurengaral is one of my most prized possessions. Her indomitable spirit and beatific smile remind me that courage comes in many forms.

paraplegia. Her legs should be amputated, the doctor said, but her mother had resisted the suggestion.

Duurengaral submitted to her treatment with a stoic calmness that hurt my heart.

She was 27 years old — she should have been at the prime of her life, working, meeting friends, falling in love. Without the means to send Duurengaral to a medical facility, her mother, too, had sacrificed everything to care for her daughter at an age when her daughter should have been taking care of her. I believe Duurengaral would not have lasted as long as she did without her mother's devotion.

When Duurengaral was diagnosed with her tumour, their lives had been changed forever. Yet here they were, smiling, uncomplaining, hospitable.

To me, their courage was unbelievable.

"She likes to sing," offered Duurengaral's mother, gazing at her daughter fondly. *Duurengaral* was Mongolian for "full of happiness" and indeed the good-natured smile had not left her face once since we arrived.

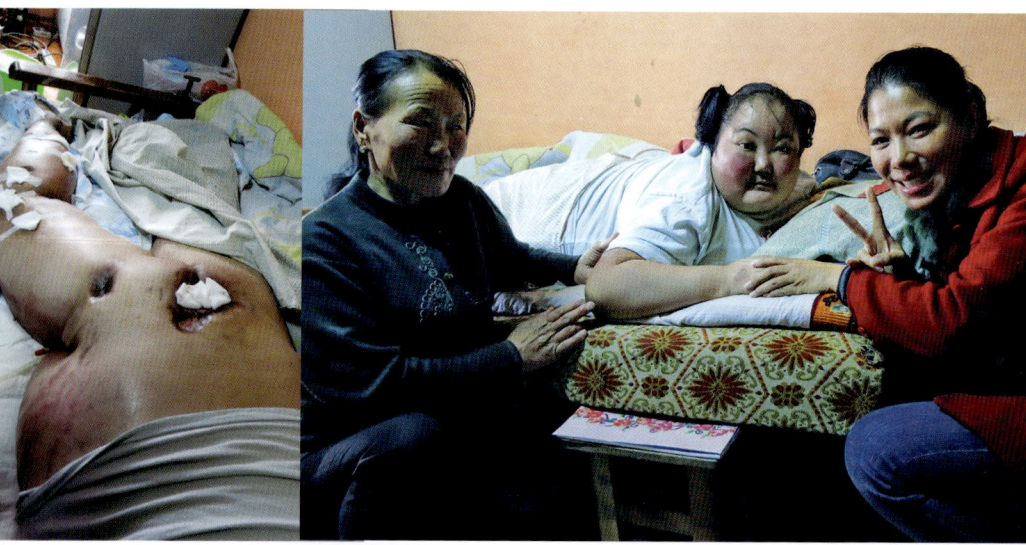

Duurengaral's bedridden state has given rise to deep pressure ulcers on her legs, back and torso, forcing her to remain perpetually on her stomach. Duurengaral's long-suffering mother (in black) is the sum of her world.

"Sing a song for us, Duurengaral!" we urged her. She gladly acquiesced, her girlish voice filling the room with melody as she sang of a mother's love for her child:

The scent of my infant body
Makes my mother content.

I see the light
Glowing from my daughter.
It is like sunlight streaming in through the window.
My infant is climbing up the windowsill
Sitting on her father's lap as though
He were her playground.

When her mother joined in the plaintive song, her voice cracking with emotion, I could not hold back my tears any longer despite my earlier resolve.

Impulsively, I gathered the mother into a hug, trying to convey the deep empathy of one woman to another.

All my walls came crashing down.

I was so ashamed of myself. In my depression I had struggled and cried and had had thoughts of ending my life. But here was Duurengaral, fighting to *stay* alive despite her loneliness, pain and disappointment.

Duurengaral was the most physically broken person I had ever seen, and I was the most emotionally broken person I had ever been.

We were two broken people struggling to keep afloat. But where she radiated with peace, I was a total mess.

Weeping openly now, I held her steady gaze and told her brokenly, "You have shown me the true meaning of courage."

Strength flowed between us as I held her hand tightly — not my strength to her, but her strength to me.

She gave me the courage to wake up, stop feeling sorry for myself and start picking up the pieces of my life. I wanted to be able to love again — not necessarily romantically, but to love my family, my friends, and those who were hurting.

***

A few months later, I heard that Duurengaral had passed away from organ failure. A group of sponsors in Malaysia were in the midst of gathering funds to fly her into the country for surgery.

Duurengaral's mother had agreed to the surgery even with the knowledge of the risks involved. I imagined the hope that the surgery held out for the stoic mother and daughter. But before the surgery could take place, Duurengaral had died.

Then last year, a chance meeting with a cameraman who had been filming in Mongolia revealed another blow: David had passed away too.

His wife, Cynthia, revealed that even before David had left for Mongolia, he had been suffering from what he jokingly called 4-in-1: high cholesterol, high blood pressure, diabetes and blocked arteries.

"Did you try to stop him from going?" I asked her.

"No, it was what he wanted," she replied quietly. "After his retirement as an engineer in the oil and gas industry, he didn't want to just sit at home and 'shake leg'. There was more that he wanted to do. He went to Mongolia to lead a meaningful life."

While in Singapore for a home visit, he had collapsed and died in the hospital.

My memories of David are still vivid: David greeting Duurengaral with his deep belly laugh and a warm clasp of the hand that conveyed more than words. David making a comical face when his staff made him try mutton. David, his face wreathed with smiles as he praised Yili, the cook at the soup kitchen, for putting so much care into the meals. David horsing around with the giggling children at the school. David with grief in his eyes as he sang *Happy Birthday* to the abandoned boy who turned another year older, all alone, at the home for destitute children.

David had a cheeky, good-humoured side, something that endeared him to his staff at Lamp of the Path even as they respected him for his professionalism and selflessness.

When I fried up some durian ice-cream balls for David as a surprise — he adored durian — he had mischievously egged his Italian co-worker to sample

Irrepressibly positive and hugely talented, hearing impaired actor and director Ramesh is much sought after in theatre circles. Bottom: A perfect day at scenic Loch Lomond.

> *There is joy to be found — joy within you, joy without, joy in all manner of relationships. Life is too short for anything less!*

some, anticipating a lot of sputtering and disgust. Instead his co-worker had enjoyed the durians! I will never forget David's comical face as his plan backfired and he had to watch his precious durian balls being gobbled up.

There were moments in Mongolia when, despite his cheerfulness, he moved a little slowly because of his heart problems. In spite of that, or perhaps because of it, he lived each day with purpose, his natural merriment turning serious only when he was fingering his prayer breads.

David and Duurengaral — both had come into my life for such a short season. But I am deeply thankful they did, because the impact they had on me was enduring.

Belinda! Live each moment with purpose, peace and love, I can almost hear them saying to me. *There is joy to be found — joy within you, joy without, joy in all manner of relationships. Life is too short for anything less!*

I will, David and Duurengaral, I promise.

Top: A durian lover, David could not get enough of the durian ice-cream balls I fried up in his kitchen from durians carted all the way from Singapore. Bottom: When I think of David I will always remember a man with one of the biggest hearts I know.

David was a big kid at heart, his wide smiles and belly laughs spreading cheer among the troubled people he fed and attended to every day. His life's motto was posted on the wall of his office.

scotland

RAMESH: MORE THAN WHOLE (I)

It was a domestic dispute. Two men were struggling against one another, each using brute strength to subdue the other. The first man viciously bent the second backward over a dining table, but the second man escaped his grasp, leaping with agility onto the dining table and dancing out of the first man's reach. Watching, their family members did nothing to try and stop them, though worry was etched on their faces.

Curiously, throughout the fight, not a word was uttered, not so much as a shout or a curse.

That was because the play, a physical theatre performance, was entirely without dialogue.

The rehearsal over, the actors relaxed. Ramesh Meyyappan, the second man, cracked a joke in sign language and his fellow actors chuckled. The air of camaraderie among the actors was unmistakable.

Ramesh, 38, is an influential and sought after theatre practitioner based in Glasgow, Scotland. He is also deaf.

The soccer game was in full swing. The sinewed boys were playing hard and fast, sparing no laggards, taking no prisoners. There was a pass, a switch, then somebody rushed up the field and... GOAL!

The boys hobbled up to each other on their crutches and high-fived, grinning widely. Some of the boys had one leg, some had none. But they were paraplegic, not powerless.

***

The dictionary defines disability as: **A physical or mental handicap, especially one that prevents a person from living a full, normal life or from holding a gainful job.**

Nothing could be more inaccurate in describing Ramesh and the Cambodian landmine victims whom I met on two separate occasions in 2012 and 2014.

But when my producer had first told me I was to interview Ramesh, I immediately began to fret. What if we couldn't communicate? What if I made a fool of myself? What if I made him feel inadequate?

On the long plane ride to Glasgow, Scotland, I had my laptop open and diligently tried to memorise a Youtube tutorial on British Sign Language.

So when Ramesh and his Scottish wife Karen Lorimer greeted me at the door of their cosy apartment, I was able to haltingly sign: *Hello, my name is B-e-l-i-n-d-a.*

I'm very impressed! signed back Ramesh encouragingly.

Ramesh, 38, had a likable, open face and an easy smile. A thoughtful, manner and scholarly glasses pegged him as an intellectual. But in the next instance, he would be mimicking a harassed driver or a demanding chef to great effect, making Karen and me laugh the entire evening. It did not take long for me to feel completely comfortable in their warm company.

Ramesh had moved to Glasgow, Scotland's largest city and Karen's hometown, six years ago. In Singapore, he had been a theatre actor and an arts educator conducting workshops for students and adults.

In Glasgow, he was a minority in more ways than one, being Asian and deaf. But seeing no reason that either should stand in the way of

Catching a subway in the historic Scottish city of Glasgow with Ramesh and Karen.

In Glasgow, he is a minority in more ways than one, being Asian and deaf. But Ramesh sees no reason that either should stand in the way of his craft.

his craft, Ramesh quickly found his place in the established world of European theatre.

His creations — an enthralling blend of physical and visual theatre using lighting, music, circus techniques, bouffon and puppetry — began to win him accolades and awards in the UK, Singapore and internationally.

Rave reviews followed his solo performances and collaborations when he went on tour across 20 countries.

The Straits Times pronounced, "Now and then you encounter an actor that just knocks you out. He makes you gasp in wonder at his craft. He reaffirms what is vital and human about theatre."

All this without his ever uttering a single word.

Ramesh has created landmark works for theatres in Sweden, London and Paris, led directing workshops, choreographed dance narratives and curated Visual Works, an event that allowed European and UK deaf artists to work with visual arts creators in Glasgow.

His influence in theatre has been nothing short of exceptional.

And through it all, not only did he treat his disability as being of little account, deafness was the very gravity that centred his professional pursuits.

To Ramesh, his deafness was no more of a disability than being born with brown eyes instead of blue.

***

When I entered the gym where he did his physical training, Ramesh was doing crunches and wriggly wrist exercises. Substituting physicality for words meant that he had to keep fit for his performances. One play had required him to stay in a half-squat for a considerable length of time. *Ouch!*

Leaping easily onto a thick rope hanging down from the ceiling, he nimbly shimmied up the rope. Aerial acrobatics was an art he had picked up two years ago to add visual interest to his performances.

Dangling three metres up in the air, he wrapped the rope around his thigh and slid his body sideways to shake my hand as I stood below watching him in fascination.

Now you try, he signed.

"Me?" I laughed. No way could I do that! But I was game to try.

Incorporating physical theatre, such as aerial acrobatics, into his performances has allowed Ramesh to express himself with his whole body.

Ziu ming ah! How does Ramesh make aerial work look so easy?

Ramesh showed me how to wrap the rope around one foot and pull myself up the rope with my arms.

What I lacked in skill, I was going to make up for in vigour. So I threw myself at the rope, assumed the stretched-out position to climb upwards and… I was stuck.

"*Ziu ming ah,* HELP!" I called out in mock distress as Ramesh and his co-actor Sita Pieraccini cracked up.

This physical theatre stuff was no joke.

***

"Isn't he great? Isn't he brilliant? That's amazing!" whispered Karen in endearing support of her husband as we sat at the back of the meeting room in House For An Art Lover.

We were observing Ramesh at a significant meeting.

He had been invited to be a member of the Programme Design Team for a ground-breaking BA Degree for Deaf at the Royal Conservatoire of Scotland, to be launched in September 2015. Input from Ramesh would help in formulating the degree programme for deaf youths.

As we observed Ramesh communicate with his hearing colleagues — sharing stories, observing attentively and making suggestions — I noticed that there was a candour and total lack of self-absorption in the way he warmly interacted with everyone and even in how he didn't think twice about wearing his favourite t-shirt and jeans ensemble to a meeting.

National Theatre of Scotland Director of Artistic Development Caroline Newall, who supports projects that challenge existing models of theatre making, wholeheartedly welcomed Ramesh's entry into Scottish theatre.

"The first time I met him, I thought he was a really talented artist who was doing something very unique in Scotland. There was no one like Ramesh in Scotland. Not only because Ramesh is deaf but also because of the kind of work that he's producing," she said. "We have a very large range of talented artists in Scotland but nobody was doing what Ramesh was doing."

His fresh approach and approachability quickly endeared him to many, both personally and professionally.

Ramesh had a way of doing away with boundaries and cutting straight to what was important — it was not important whether this was a Singaporean or a Scottish stage, it was important to push the boundaries of theatre in imaginative ways. It was not important whether he was Asian or Caucasian, it was important that he was professional. It did not matter whether he was deaf or hearing, it mattered that he had something unique to contribute to the craft he loved.

The National Theatre of Scotland whole-heartedly welcomed Ramesh's involvement in Scottish theatre.

***

As a couple, Ramesh and Karen complemented each other like curry and *chapatti*. Going to the supermarket, where Ramesh needed to pick up some Indian spices for dinner, turned out to be lots of laughs as they attempted to teach me how to sign "soap" and "carrot" and "apple" as we roamed the aisles, picking up produce and groceries. Goofy as always, I hazarded a guess as to how "chicken breast" was signed, much to Ramesh and Karen's amusement.

> **It did not matter whether he was deaf or hearing, it mattered that he had something unique to contribute to the craft he loved.**

It turned out that Ramesh was not only skilled on stage, he was terrific in the kitchen, expertly producing curries and stir-fried vegetables and crunchy *pappadam* for our dinner.

"I try to get in the kitchen with him, but I just get in the way," Karen quipped. "We argue about two things in life: driving and cooking."

At the topic of driving, Ramesh comically sucked in his breath, arched his eyebrows and mock elbowed me in a conspiratorial nudge.

"Hey," laughed Karen. "I'll admit that you cook better than I do. But you need to admit that I drive better than you!"

Ramesh's 12-year-old, pink rice cooker was the subject of much hilarity. His mother had bought it for him when he had left for university in the UK years ago and he had kept it since. It was one of his most prized possessions.

"That rice cooker came before I did," said Karen. "I'm jealous of its pinkness."

"What if one day your precious rice cooker stops working?" I teased Ramesh.

He cooks too! Ramesh's pink rice cooker, a gift from his mother when he was a university student, is one of his prized possessions.

I'll ask my mother to send me another one, he signed and mimed a rice cooker hopping its way from Singapore to Scotland and himself opening up the box like an excited kid at Christmas.

A home-cooked meal with these two felt like being among old friends.

It was amazing how quiet the room became when Ramesh was not in it, even though we never heard his voice.

Beyond all the teasing and joking, I admired Karen's skill at interpreting for Ramesh. Considerately, she signed every question and answer, never presuming to reply for him but respecting that he had a voice although he had no words.

Her loyal support of Ramesh must have played a big role in how seamlessly he had settled into Glasgow.

***

By the fourth day of our filming, Ramesh and I were having animated conversations at the back of the car as Karen drove us to the spectacular Loch Lomond for a picnic. To his credit, Ramesh never made fun of my clumsy attempts at conversing with him.

Loch Lomond, the largest lake in Great Britain by surface area, is a vast, serene lake overlooked by the gently rolling Scottish Highlands. Ramesh

The scenic Scottish countryside provides a peaceful setting for our filming.

Filming an interview over a picturesque picnic. The only trouble was, my producer had picked a spot that was plagued with flies! If you watch the episode closely, you will see Ramesh constantly swatting at the pesky flies!

and Karen walked hand in hand as we strolled along the lakeside, admiring charming stone cottages with blossoms creeping up the walls.

Sitting down for a picnic in a grassy patch along a woodland trail, Karen related the story of how they had come to settle in Glasgow.

"I had arrived in Singapore to teach and I was to work with Ramesh. My boss said, 'This is Ramesh. He's a deaf Indian. Go and get to know one another.' I knew nothing about sign language at the time but picked it up simply by working alongside Ramesh. Before I left Singapore I took a sign language exam at the deaf institute and actually passed!"

"You're a genius!" I kidded her. "Were there any challenges in your relationship?"

Karen repeated the question in sign language for Ramesh. He raised his eyebrows and tapped his fists together to express conflict.

"My parents are from India, and according to Indian culture they expected me to have an Indian wife," interpreted Karen as Ramesh signed energetically. "I don't quite understand why. To me race isn't important. It's about communication with a person rather than race."

When Karen's father fell ill, Ramesh had urged Karen to return to Scotland as her family needed her. When she left Singapore, he had left with her.

"I respected him for doing that for me," said Karen. "At one point I had three family members in hospital, which made his decision even more brave because I didn't have time for Ramesh when we got to Scotland. It showed the commitment that he had to our relationship. So emotionally he made me feel that he cared, that he wanted our relationship to work no matter what. That was massive to me."

"How do you feel about your marriage now?" I asked.

"Well I'm disappointed that he's lost his hair. He's not the same Ramesh that I fell for," Karen deadpanned as we cracked up. "Seriously, I feel that he's made life interesting for sure."

Looking into Ramesh's eyes, she signed, *I love your passion about things. There's an honesty about you as a person. We see that when you communicate.*

Ramesh wasn't the only half of the couple who was authentic. There was a genuineness about them both that made me want to get to know them better.

Karen has been Ramesh's most ardent supporter and capable interpreter ever since they met as colleagues in Singapore.

When the two were married, Ramesh had been easily absorbed into Karen's family and social circle, some of whom we met that evening when we were invited to dinner at a friend's home.

We had a full serving of Scottish hospitality at a table laden with pies, turnips, prawns, salmon, potatoes, steamed veggies and… *gulp*… haggis. Yes it really is an animal's stomach stuffed with sheep's heart, liver, lungs, oatmeal and spices, served up in all its unadorned, gutsy glory. What can I say — we have durian, the Scottish have haggis!

Ramesh, naturally sociable, was as comfortable with Karen's family and friends as he was with his theatre colleagues.

In this day and age when many of us spend way too much time looking at our electronic devices, a conversation with him was unusually personal. A mindful gaze and attentiveness were all we needed for a good, old-fashioned conversation.

***

Just before we left Scotland, my camera crew and I were in for a treat. We were going to watch Ramesh perform his celebrated production *Snails & Ketchup*.

The famous Scottish hospitality showed itself by way of a generous meal laid out by Ramesh and Karen's friends, including the infamous haggis! (top left)

Originally commissioned for *Unlimited*, a project celebrating disability, arts, culture and sport as part of London's 2012 Cultural Olympiad, tonight the stunning performance created by Ramesh was being performed in Glasgow as part of the Surge festival organised by Conflux, which promoted street art, physical theatre and circus art.

I paid a visit to Ramesh backstage before the show.

"Shall we film you stripping?" I teased him.

No! he signed and mimed the slamming of a door and the fastening of a long row of locks, much to my amusement.

"Are you nervous?" I asked.

Yes, he signed. *But when I get on stage, I become completely focused.*

How did I understand that so clearly without knowing sign language? He really was a master communicator.

Sitting with Karen in the audience, we held our breath as the lights dimmed and the play began.

The darkly comic story followed the son of a dysfunctional family as he took to the trees to live an arboreal existence to escape a brutal home environment.

A curtain of hanging ropes provided an ingenious, three-dimensional set.

I was riveted as Ramesh parted the ropes and emerged, all angular elbows and knees like a graceful spider. Now he was tiptoeing in exaggerated slow motion. Now he was being spanked over an oversized dining chair. Now he was escaping to the sanctuary of a tree (one of the ropes) where he sat with the melancholy expression of a boy yearning to escape. He made eating an imaginary apple enthralling, so powerful was his artistry.

At the end, I had tears in my eyes from his wrenching performance. I could hear the audience members around me remarking on how poetic he was, how moved they were, how he was a one-of-a-kind actor.

***

Ramesh's career is impressive for any theatre professional, not to mention a professional with a disability. He had me thinking: What do I view as my disability? The albatross around my neck? My excuse for not reaching further, dreaming bigger, living larger?

This humble, genuine, talented man showed me that a disability accepted, rather than dreaded, can turn out to be no disability at all.

> **This humble, genuine, talented man showed me that a disability accepted, rather than dreaded, can turn out to be no disability at all.**

Volunteer Zenn (top left) and her best friend Om, whose deep friendship needs no words.
wBottom: A young amputee playing on the swings at Arrupe Centre in Cambodia.

cambodia

LANDMINE VICTIMS: MORE THAN WHOLE (II)

Two years after I met Ramesh, my camera crew and I filmed some boys and girls who lived halfway across the world from him, but who embodied the same buoyant spirit.

We were in Battambang, Cambodia, to film Zenn Tan, 37, a Singaporean graphic designer who had been volunteering at the Arrupe Centre for the past three years. The centre, a refuge for children and youths who were victims of polio or landmine accidents, had been founded by Spanish priest Enrique "Kike" Figaredo, also affectionately known as the "Bishop of the Wheelchairs".

Three decades of civil war had left Cambodia with a landscape littered with dangerous landmines, especially in rural areas. Over 64,000 landmine casualties have been recorded in Cambodia since 1979, and with an estimated 40,000 *chon pika*, or amputees, Cambodia has the highest ratio of amputees per capita in the world.

Bishop Kike (left) set up Arrupe when he was approached to create a centre for Cambodia's young polio and landmine victims. He welcomed Zenn (right) as a volunteer even though she had not initially known how she could help. Bottom: The landscaped garden at Arrupe is a picture of tranquility.

One third of the casualties are children, especially boys, as it has been found that males are more likely than females to pick up explosives.

With little governmental aid or access to good healthcare, many low income victims have been devastated by the landmines which Pol Pot, head of the genocidal Khmer Rouge regime, once called his "perfect soldiers" because of their deadly efficacy. Battambang had one of the highest incidences of landmine accidents.

From the road, Arrupe Centre was hidden from view. A thicket of tall trees towered behind the yellow brick walls that ringed the compound. So when our taxi drove through the gates, past the trees and up the dirt driveway into the expansive, park-like compound, it was like discovering a secret garden.

As we got out of our taxi, Zenn and two smiling boys stepped forward. The older boy, who looked about 12, was leaning lightly on a crutch. He had only one leg. Together the boys presented me with a peach-coloured *krama*, a traditional Cambodian scarf that covered a multitude of uses including carrying a baby and wrapping the face on dusty country roads.

"Wow, I get a gift as soon as I arrive!" I quipped, beaming.

Zenn, slim and neat and wearing a striped *krama* around her neck, was close to my age but had a motherly air from caring for the boys and girls at Arrupe.

"Let's go inside where it's cooler," she said.

The double-storey building of cool concrete with arched windows was welcoming after the searing heat outside.

Lemon-yellow walls decorated with colourful artwork, checkerboard floor tiles of white and ochre, and old-fashioned standing fans gave the place a homely air. One wall was covered with a mural of villagers relaxing in a garden bordered by flowers and ferns stretching all the way to where the green horizon met the blue sky. The whole place had the kind of organic flow and peacefulness that cheered the heart.

Wheelchaired children were bent over wooden desks, absorbed in story books. In other corners of the capacious room, a group of older teens, also in wheelchairs, were being coached by an academic tutor.

Neatly dressed and combed, the boys and girls were like boys and girls the world over — fresh faced and with a youth's anticipatory gleam in eyes not yet jaded by cynicism.

The difference was only apparent when you looked at their limbs. Some of them had legs amputated at the knees, others had legs that were permanently twisted or had wasted away to sticks. I honestly had never seen this many young people in wheelchairs in one place. They had lost their legs when they had accidentally stepped on landmines. They had lost their arms when they had picked up mines to examine or play with, not comprehending the danger.

The landmine victims lead as full a life as most children, many of them attending school in town.

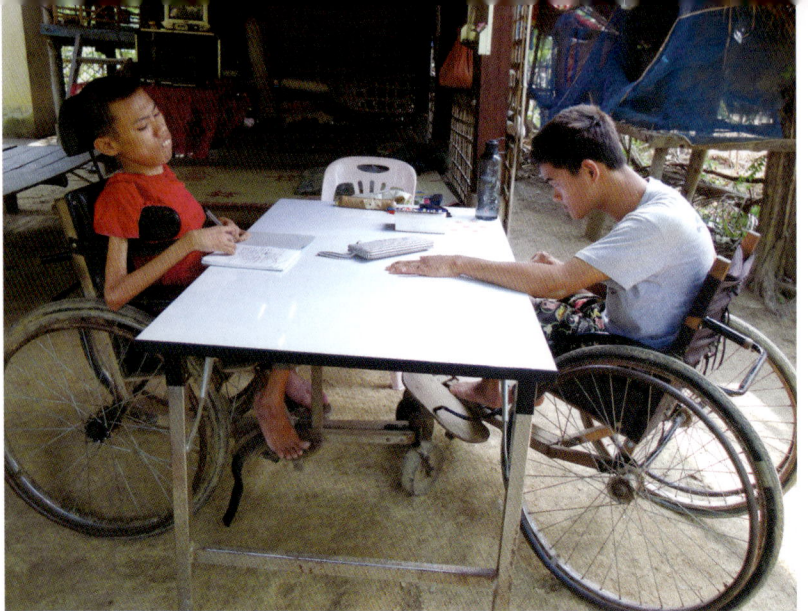

The centre provides academic coaching for its student residents.

***

Arrupe had been started in 1998 when a group of NGOs had approached Bishop Kike to create a centre for disabled children who needed a home.

When I met the white haired bishop with the benevolent smile who still lives in and runs the centre, he explained, "The NGOs told me, 'We have many disabled children who need rehabilitation and education and they have no means in their village.' So initially I designed a little centre for 15, just 15, and now we have over 50."

Kike had joined the Jesuits as a 20 year old studying economics in Madrid. Upon his graduation, he had signed up as a volunteer with the Jesuit Refugee Service and arrived at the Thai-Cambodian border where nearly half a million Cambodian refugees were living cheek by jowl after fleeing from their war-torn country.

In an interview with jesuitmission.org.au, Kike said the Cambodians, especially those who had been maimed by landmines and who "in their bodies were carrying the wounds of war" touched him deeply and he encouraged them to reconnect with their traditional dance and music, outlawed in Cambodia because "it was the symbol of the royal palace and of the things Khmer Rouge did not want for their people".

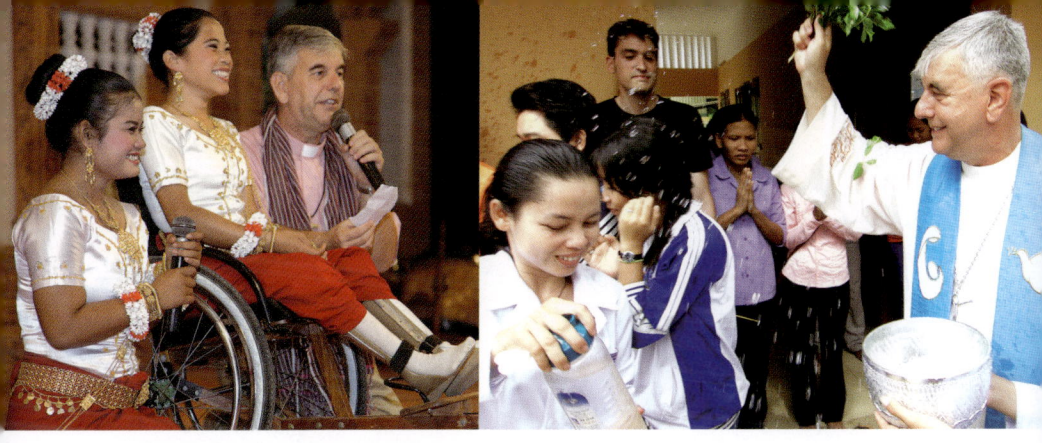

A traditional Cambodian dance troupe consisting of amputees (left) frequently performs at local celebrations over which the genial Bishop Kike presides.

When the Jesuits decided to work in Cambodia in 1988, Kike raised his hand again.

"The country was collapsed by the war and division… It was very difficult to do planning, to make development, to help the needs of the poor. There were curfews, checkpoints, guns everywhere," recalled Kike. But he undertook to understand "the hearts of the people who were hurt by all those years of war" by living among them and sharing the same life and language.

Arrupe was set up to give young polio and landmine victims rehabilitative treatment, wheelchairs, prosthetics and education. Optional activities include a dance programme where 150 children perform traditional dances incorporating wheelchairs and crutches.

"The children go to school in their wheelchairs. They give so much light and beauty to our place. In fact I think the compound of the Catholic Church in Battambang is very special thanks to them," said Kike, now the Bishop of Battambang leading 26 Catholic communities.

***

When Zenn had approached Bishop Kike saying, "I would like to volunteer here at Arrupe for six months but I don't know what I can offer", he had told her, "Don't worry, you come and you offer your friendship, your kindness and we will start to get your gifts."

Six months became three years, and Zenn indeed found her place in Arrupe. Using her artistic flair in the souvenir shop, she painted a charming

Handicrafts sold at Arrupe are made by local craftsmen, including the outfit I am wearing as I cook laksa as a special treat for Zenn! The Jesus figure on the wooden heart (bottom right) shows Jesus with one leg shorter than the other as a reminder that He died on the cross for the disabled as well.

mural of willow trees blowing in the wind and helped with merchandising at the shop selling wooden crosses, scarves, postcards, clothing and knick knacks in support of handicapped craftspeople from Phnom Penh and Siem Reap.

But it was really in her role as a "den mother" to the 24 nine to 24 year olds in the boys' house that she found her calling.

We found the boys engaged in a lively game of soccer in the open space in front of their house. An older boy leaned on a crutch while expertly kicking a ball with a mighty *thwack*. The ball sailed over to his opponents who lunged for it in their crutches.

At a far corner, another group was lawn bowling, the most enthusiastic among them being a boy of about 16 whose legs were twisted out in opposite directions and whose right arm was permanently bent behind his back.

As I admired the athleticism of the boys, a wheelchair passed by, its occupant maneuvering expertly up a curb of bricks and down again on the other side.

"Can I try?" I asked, wanting to know how it felt to live, work and play in a wheelchair.

The wheelchairs were not high-tech by any means. Designed for activity, they had two larger wheels on the side and a rudimentary wooden baseboard that led to a small wheel in front. Completely manual, they had to be manoeuvred using sheer arm strength.

I could hardly fit into the tiny seat and when I did, rolling the wheelchair forward with my arms for just a metre in the pebbly dirt path made me pant with exertion.

Undeterred, I tried navigating the brick curb. Zenn had to help me up and I foolishly attempted to roll down the curb on my own, only managing to tip to the side and tumble off with a shriek. The boys and girls had made this look deceptively easy!

Dusting myself off with a laugh and restoring the wheelchair to its rightful owner, I joined an ongoing game of hand *chatek* with a ponytailed girl who smoothly spun on her crutches, her eyes shining with fun. These youths were such good company, I was thoroughly enjoying my time with them.

"Do you play like this all the time?" I asked a tall boy by the name of Mony who spoke a little English.

"Oh no," Mony replied. "We have classes in the morning, then in the afternoon we help out in the garden. We play when we have time."

Zenn interrupted, "We're having a party here tonight. The younger children will be returning to their village for the holidays tomorrow and we are also celebrating the end of exams for the older children."

All around us the youths, both girls and boys, were preparing for the celebratory dinner. Three amputees were sweeping the yard with brooms, while others were splitting sugarcane or setting up round wooden tables. Another had a crate of Coca-Cola bottles on his lap which he rolled in his wheelchair to the buffet table.

The kitchen was all a-bustle — two youths were peeling ginger, slicing onions and dicing chicken at a counter that was lowered to facilitate their wheelchairs. Another fried up a great wok-full of meat and vegetables, piling the food on huge aluminium trays for his friends to wheel out to the buffet table.

Young amputees and polio victims throw themselves into energetic games of soccer after school, while others prefer the bicycles or the swings.

The scene was amazing. These youths, tackling their tasks with efficiency, good humour and purpose, defied pity.

Maimed and robbed of a rosy future through no fault of their own, their life was not going to be an easy one. Many low-income landmine victims struggled to get stable jobs and ended up hawking snacks in the city where they were frowned upon.

Yet all around me the teens were laughing and chatting, not one dour face among them. Despite being broken in body, they were more content and more "whole" than many disgruntled youths I have seen in first world countries.

Tucking in to the feast whipped up by many cheerful hands, I gamely answered a barrage of questions by the boys at my table on life in Singapore. They were handsome boys, their faces the deep colour of the tamarind fruit that they enjoyed snacking on.

The effects of Arrupe on these vulnerable youths was clear. Despite their disability these boys and girls, who studied in primary and high schools in town, had a close community of like-minded friends to return to at the end of the day. Here they had buddies to play rowdy games with and den mothers like Zenn to confide in. A few youths who had grown up at Arrupe have moved to Phnom Penh where they were studying at a university or undergoing vocation training.

Zenn clearly adored her charges, conversing easily with them in Khmer and listening to their chatter attentively. Her desire was to help them develop a healthy emotional and mental core so that they could live out the rest of their lives with the same heart and drive as other youths.

Introducing me to a handsome boy of 15 or 16 with wavy hair and a silver chain around his neck, a Cambodian Justin Bieber, Zenn said, "He is our newest resident. Just last year he had been walking along the same path he walked every day when he stepped on a landmine. At first he thought it was just his feet that were injured, but he had to have both legs amputated."

"You know, these boys don't seem helpless at all," I said to Zenn.

Her face softened as she gazed at her chattering boys. "A lot of people come here ready to pity them… so *ke lian*, so pitiful. When you come with

Wheelchair-bound residents sweep the grounds and prepare for a barbeque.

this attitude, you can't see what they are capable of. But living here among them, I can tell you, they are the accomplished ones and I am the helpless one!

"I remember when I first arrived, there was an exceptional boy in the school. One day he came up to me and said, 'Can you tell me what I can do?' I said to him, 'I should be the one asking you what you can do. What can you help me with or help yourself with?' From that day on, the two of us have competed to see who can help who the most!"

She patted a young man on the shoulder. "Makara, he's 23, he used to help me too. The road outside the compound used to be a mud road, almost impassable to cars. When it rained, I would take 15 minutes just to travel on my motorcycle a few meters. The boys, including Makara, would go out and help me get out of the mud and take me home."

I turned to Makara. "So you always take care of Zenn when she's here?"

"Ya," he said bashfully.

"His expression is fierce but that's because he's very shy," said Zenn fondly.

"You are Zenn's superhero," I teased him.

"Thank you," he replied softly.

Who says gallantry is dead? These boys, despite having lost a leg or an arm, were always ready to help a person in need.

But one boy in particular had a special place in Zenn's heart. Om, an intellectually disabled boy in his 20s who was unable to push his own wheelchair because both his feet and hands were twisted, had come to Arrupe's notice when a hospital had called the centre.

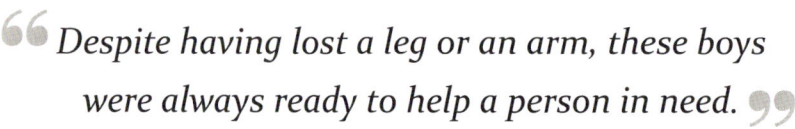

Despite having lost a leg or an arm, these boys were always ready to help a person in need.

A man had died in the hospital, leaving behind a son with no one to care for him, they said. When the Arrupe staff visited the hospital, they saw that Om needed help, and they brought him back to the centre.

"Why is Om special to you?" I asked her.

Zenn replied, "When I first arrived in Battambang, I didn't speak the language, so I couldn't communicate with people. But this boy was a boy of few words and he would quietly sit behind or beside me and watch me work, keeping me company."

How did they communicate then? I wondered. My answer came when I saw Zenn doing a wheelchair dance with Om. Pushing his wheelchair

Om, who does not speak, came to the attention of Arrupe Centre when they received a call saying a man had died in hospital, leaving a son who needed help. It is clear from the way he looks at Zenn that they share a special bond..

this way and that, backwards and in circles, Zenn did her little wheelchair waltz as if to a secret tune in her head, knowing that Om would feel her compassion in every spin and her affection in every whirl.

Om, an orphan without family or home or voice, had found a kindred spirit in Zenn that went beyond the need for words.

I saw then that sometimes a profound friendship can be built upon the unspoken things. It was one of the sweetest friendships I have ever witnessed.

***

Zenn and Om have formed an unlikely but beautiful friendship based on trust and affection.

During a Catholic festival that was being celebrated in the compound, I watched a dance of a different kind.

Scores of worshippers started flowing through the gates to the Catholic church from an early hour.

As Bishop Kike, in his ceremonial white robe, conducted the service in Khmer, a line of little girls as young as five stood to one side, their dimpled hands pressed together in prayer.

At the end of the service, Aruppe's dance troupe stepped up to perform — 10 lovely young ladies who wore Cambodian costumes with pleated swathes of jade green, sapphire blue or ruby red cloth draped femininely over one shoulder. Half of them were in wheelchairs. But all of them bore the grace of age-old tradition as they delicately turned their wrists and arched their fingers to the beat and hum and tinkle of Khmer drums, bells and bamboo instruments.

This was one dance I would never forget.

***

At Arrupe, some of the female students attend classes on traditional dance and give performances incorporating wheelchairs and crutches.

On our last day of filming, Zenn announced that we were going on an excursion to a village two hours' drive away.

"These are three of our workers: Pu Sor, Pu Tav and Rith," she introduced two men in their 40s and 50s (hence the prefix Pu as a mark of respect to an elder) and a 24-year-old young lady. "Without them we would have no children at the centre because they are the ones who go out to the villages to identify children in need."

Pu Sor drove us in an open-backed pick-up truck, and I was glad for the *krama* wrapped around my face, as the truck kicked up great clouds of dust. Despite the scarf, dust was getting into my eyes and my nose and my mouth and I had to move into the front cab with Pu Sor.

It was a good thing I did, because a moment later, the truck accidentally ran over a slithering snake on the road. Pu Sor halted the truck immediately. This snake was a delicacy and finding a snake was like finding gold.

A farmer ran out onto the road and proceeded to argue with Pu Sor over the rightful ownership of the snake. Pu Sor must have won because I saw him running back to the truck with the snake which he hurled into the back — *piang!* I have a phobia of snakes and when I saw the huge snake in the back of the truck, still wriggling, I gave a squeal to wake the dead. Ignoring me, Pu Sor looked pleased. He would present the snake to the villagers — it was a great gift!

Along the bumpy dirt road to the village, we passed a wheelchair-vehicle with three large wheels and pedals at the handlebars operated by hand, its driver pedalling energetically. The ingenuity of the Cambodians is amazing.

Our destination was a village called Prey Thom (big forest), set among flat, green fields.

We were about to set off down a mud path to visit one of the villagers when Zenn clutched my arm and said, "Belinda, this is a mine field."

"*What?*" I choked out.

"Don't worry," Zenn smiled. "Pu Sor told me that in 2005 this whole area was bought by our organisation. From 2006, we started clearing out the landmines and gave plots to landless families to farm and live in safety."

Sarod and Phalla, a young husband and his disabled wife, and two young children, were one of the families living in Prey Thom. Their traditional

In Cambodia, where 64,000 landmine casualties have been recorded since 1979, danger lurks in every innocuous-looking road.

Cambodian hut on stilts had walls of dried leaves and a floor of bamboo posts. We sat in hammocks and stools in the cool communal space below the hut, the children watching us curiously.

"Has it made a difference in your life to have a home to call your own?" I asked the young husband and father.

"We are much happier," he said in a soft voice. "Before, with no land, we had to beg people for help. Now we can work our own land and feed our children."

As we left the family to make our way back to Arrupe, Zenn nodded to Pu Sor and said, "Pu Sor is one of my heroes, you know. He and many of our workers work part-time at the centre for as little as US$100 a month. Although he can earn more elsewhere, he works with us because he is a landmine victim too. Both his legs are prosthetic."

With his steady gait and capable driving, I would never have believed it had Pu Sor not proceeded to raise the hem of his pants up to his knees, revealing a pair of fiberglass prosthetic legs, though his feet were in regular socks and shoes.

"Does working at Arrupe mean a lot to you?" I asked him with new respect.

"Yes," he said simply in Khmer. "We are not a business or a factory, we are a big family. And family members need to help each other. Even though I am just one person and handicapped, I have the chance to help others and if I can help 20 children, they can help 20 more."

***

Many of us travel to foreign lands to admire physical beauty: the scenery, the flora and the fauna. But the landmine victims I met in Cambodia, Zenn, Bishop Kike, Pu Sor, and Ramesh in Glasgow… they took me on a spiritual journey.

Through them I now see what it means to be whole, not necessarily physically, but in spirit.

> *Even though I am just one person and handicapped, I have the chance to help others and if I can help 20 children, they can help 20 more.*

> *Through them I now see what it means to be whole, not necessarily physically, but in spirit.*

Top: This is a special spot for Michael and Jacqueline — they have taken a picture here every wedding anniversary and have seen the face of Hanoi changing through the photos. Sixteen-year-old Grace (centre) has grown up in Hanoi and considers this her home.

vietnam

MICHAEL: CAFÉ COUNSELLOR

Do you believe we all have a calling? Something we, and only we with our unique set of characteristics, experiences and passions, are meant to fulfill in our lives?

I asked myself this question after meeting all the remarkable men and women in this book.

Ravi rescuing broken children who were discarded by their own families.

Fang Fang risking life and limb to bring comfort to isolated mountain dwellers.

Joe capturing elusive dreams and turning them into reality.

One-legged Cambodian boys playing soccer with the zeal of Ronaldinho.

Ramesh expressing volumes without words.

Nicholas describing the shape of hope to boys caught in a cycle of hopelessness.

They are larger than life to me not just because they have the heart of giants. They are larger than life to me because they have risen above the things that could have weighed them down — poverty, timidity, disability — in order to fulfill their life's purpose.

***

Michael Ong, 45, was one of those who began thinking about his calling at a very young age.

His family lived in a one-room rental flat in Tanjung Rhu in the 1970s. Struggling to make ends meet, his mother peddled bleach and detergent diluted with water. His father was a seaman whom he did not have recollections of until he was 16.

When Michael was conceived, the youngest of seven children, his mother consulted a *sinseh* for ways to abort him. She already had six mouths to feed and had no means to feed another. But despite her attempts at self abortion, Michael survived.

At his birth, the family could not afford to go to the hospital, so he was delivered at home. His grandmother took on the role of midwife, and through inexperience, Michael almost suffocated to death. But he survived.

At primary one, he was walking with his mother one day when she pointed to another schoolboy his age and said, "See that boy? He substituted for you."

"What do you mean?" a puzzled seven-year-old Michael asked.

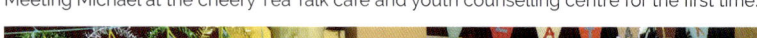

Meeting Michael at the cheery Tea Talk café and youth counselling centre for the first time.

"Before you were born, we had decided to give you away to another family. But then you turned out to be a boy, more valuable, so we kept you. That is why your name is Kek Hin — Hin sounds like *heng* because you were so lucky! That boy was given away to that family instead. *Heng ah!*"

Young Michael mused over what he heard and pondered the meaning of all this.

He saw how his mother struggled to put food on the table and provide her children with an education. His older sister began giving tuition when she was 12 years old so that she did not have to take a single cent from their mother.

"I began to ask myself: what is my life all about?" said Michael. "I almost got aborted. I almost died at birth. I was almost sold. So growing up in a poor family played a big part in my decision to study social work and psychology when I went to the National University of Singapore."

He marked his university graduation with a trip to Vietnam with a group of friends that included his future wife, Jacqueline.

"That was when my heart was broken for the Vietnamese people," Michael said. "I saw children, orphans, begging for money. I saw people with disabilities rolling on trolleys in the street, using their hands to push themselves. Partly because of my background, growing up poor, and partly because of my training as a social worker, I felt that there was so much need to be met for the Vietnamese people. But I didn't know how."

The answer came in a dream.

"One night I dreamt that I invited five Vietnamese friends to my home. But these five invited another five, and those five invited another five, and another five and on and on," said Michael. "In my dream, I remember welcoming them, shaking their hands, but as they kept coming and coming, my feelings of hospitality turned into hostility. I was angry, thinking, 'I only have energy for quality relationships with five of you. Why do you keep coming?'

"Then I heard a voice saying: *Michael, look into their eyes.* And as I shook their hands, I looked into each person's eyes, and I saw that this one had been abused, this one had been raped, this one was a drug addict, this one was lonely and hurt. And in my dream I started crying.

"That was an important point in my life. I realised that the Vietnamese people had internal needs and that the healing of the heart is just as important as the healing of the body."

But when Michael, then 25, suggested to Jacqueline the possibility of moving to Vietnam, she was taken aback. *Did she really want to give up her life in Singapore?* So doubtful was she that she even considered breaking up with Michael.

"Jacqueline wasn't keen on the idea of going to Vietnam. And while I was very keen, I was more keen on her!" said Michael, chuckling at the recollection. "We had met on the bus on the way to our first day of school at Tampines Junior College. It was raining and being a typical boy I had not brought an umbrella. Jacqueline's older sister, who was accompanying her to school, shared her umbrella with me and introduced me to her little sister. That was how our friendship began! So I had known Jacqueline since we were both 17… how could I give up our eight-year relationship for a dream?"

When Michael, his wife Jacqueline and toddler Grace moved to Hanoi, they had planned to do voluntary work for a year. Fourteen years later, they are still living and working amongst the Vietnamese, whom they have grown to love.

He decided that he would not push the issue. The two were married and had a beautiful baby daughter, Grace. And the matter was not brought up again.

…Until there was another dream. This time it was Jacqueline's.

"Although Michael had stopped talking about Vietnam, I felt that he carried a certain sadness about him, that there was something missing in his life," Jacqueline recalled.

"Then one night I had a dream. I dreamt that I died and went to heaven and there I met God, who asked me: *Do you know why Michael is not going to Vietnam?* I said: *Why?* And God said: *Because of you.*

"I woke up with a heavy heart. I knew that as a wife I should not be standing in the way of my husband's calling. I don't know how I had the courage, but I went to him and asked, 'Do you still want to go to Vietnam?' And he said, 'Yes.' So I said, '*Hao ba.* Okay, we shall go for one year.'"

Fourteen years later, Michael, Jacqueline and Grace, now 16, are still in Vietnam.

***

Michael and Jacqueline live like the locals, travelling everywhere by scooter.

Tea Talk has become a sanctuary for local youths, who meet here for a meal and sometimes a listening ear.

Flying to Hanoi was an easy three-hour journey compared to some of the trips my camera crew and I had taken. But I knew that there were always surprises during my travelogue filming and although this was my fourth time in Vietnam, I wondered what excitement this trip would spring on us.

True to its status as a developing country, Vietnam had certainly developed since I first visited 13 years ago. At that time, Hanoi had been a sleepy backwater with mostly bicycle traffic.

This time it was 2014 and walking down a Hanoi street was a little more harrowing. Narrow shophouses with worn awnings squeezed up against one another, hawking mobile phones and other electronics. Main roads flanked by the gracious arches of French architecture were overrun by blaring, beeping, revving, weaving vans, taxis, trishaws and an endless wave of motorbikes, their riders masked against the choking pollution.

But every now and then I caught sight of a vendor on foot pushing a cart bristling with brooms of all kinds, or a sidewalk stall selling steaming noodles deftly cooked by a woman in a conical hat. And it felt like the old Vietnam I knew.

***

I found Michael's café, Tea Talk, in an uncharacteristically quiet side street shaded by spreading trees.

Set in a pretty, balconied building with French influences, the café was a welcome oasis after the cacophonous din of the main roads. Inside, the walls were painted in warm shades of mustard, cherry and apple. Round cafe tables, sofas, curtained windows, bookshelves and cookie jars gave the place a homey air.

Michael and Jacqueline had specially designed the café to have a welcoming feel because it was not just a café. It was also a counselling centre for youths between 18 and 30.

Tea Talk was born out of data that showed that, because of factors such as the Vietnam War, the median age of Vietnamese was just 26, with almost a third of the population consisting of 15 to 29 year olds.

Many young people were deprived of parental guidance, or could not bridge the generation gap between their traditional village parents and the liberal, modern-day demands and temptations of urban Hanoi.

Social problems such as mental health issues, HIV AIDs and domestic violence were rife. The youth needed guidance, they needed counselling, they needed a moral compass.

But there was a severe shortage of social workers in Vietnam — in 2010 Time magazine reported that 60,000 social workers were needed in the next decade just to attain a ratio of one social worker to 10,000 Vietnamese.

There was also a stigma associated with seeking help from counsellors and social workers.

Michael was convinced that he needed to reach out to youths to help heal their internal pain. He had seen too many fall into depression and harbour suicidal thoughts.

The café was a non-threatening platform to not only meet with youths who needed counseling, but also train them to help their peers.

***

When I walked into Tea Talk, it was choc-a-block with lively tertiary-aged boys and girls, helping themselves to cupcakes, cookies and, of course, tea.

"Hi Belinda, welcome, welcome," greeted Michael, a trim, bespectacled man with a pleasant voice and an easy smile. He looked like he could be Vietnamese, so comfortable was he in his surroundings. In fact, Michael spoke Vietnamese fluently, together with English, Mandarin, Cantonese and his native Hokkien.

"*Wah*, is it always this packed?" I asked him.

"Well there's a party tonight," replied Michael. "We are celebrating the graduation of our Let's Talk course participants."

A 10-week Let's Talk course for youths aged 18 to 22 allowed them to pick up basic counselling skills.

"After the course, they are tasked to play the role of a paracounsellor for the next three months," Michael said. "We don't use these technical terms — we just say, okay now you are a Let's Talker and you are equipped with basic counseling skills. When you are at home, at school, at the playground or wherever you go about life and you encounter someone in need who longs for a listening ear, you offer help."

The instant popularity of Let's Talk spoke of a desperate longing among the Vietnamese youth.

Michael had expected about 40 youths to register when he publicised the first course at schools and university campuses around the neighbourhood. To his surprise, 150 applied for the 20 places.

He found out why when the youths starting opening up.

"My students are around 20 years old, which makes their parents between 40 and 60," said Michael. "If you trace Vietnam's history, their parents would have been children during or just after the Vietnam War. During that era people did not have the benefit of parental guidance and violence was a common way to deal with domestic disputes.

"I've spoken to some women in their 60s and 70s who told me what it was like during the war. One woman said that as a young mother she had to walk many kilometres to work her fields and find food each day. Before she left home, she would place some food on the floor for her young children who were of crawling age. When she returned at the end of the day she would sometimes see them eating their own faeces.

"Another woman was a child during the war and, as there was no adult to look after her while her mother was out working and foraging, she was chained up all day until the mother returned."

Not surprisingly, when these damaged women were faced with raising their young adult children in a completely different social era, the challenges loomed.

"Young people in their 20s and below have developed Western ideas of individuality which are at odds with traditional Vietnamese family values," said Michael. "They want to pursue their dream and their parents say cannot. They want to study in this university and their parents say cannot. They want to love this girl, and their parents say cannot. It's a bit like watching a Korean drama playing out in front of you! But the conflicts are very real."

So even as the youths in the Let's Talk programme learn how to help their peers, they are learning how to help themselves.

One of his Let's Talk youths, Tra My, had grown from being a participant in the first programme, to a translator in the second, a co-teacher in the third and an independent teacher in the fourth.

She had been a final-year university student, assigned to Michael as a teaching assistant during a social work course he conducted for government officials.

At the end of their three-day course, she surprised him by saying, "I had already decided to quit social work when I graduated but you have rekindled my passion for social work."

Today Tra My is working with women who have been trafficked.

***

Despite the popularity of the café, Tea Talk had not been in Michael's plans when he had first arrived in Vietnam. He had started out as a volunteer with non-governmental organisation Resource Exchange International (REI) which sends professionals from different fields into developing countries. Michael volunteered at Hanoi's University of Labour and Social Affairs as a social work lecturer.

A night of smiles and sharing as young men and women celebrate their graduation from Michael's Let's Talk basic counselling programme.

At the time Jacqueline was a stay-at-home mum who indulged Michael's penchant for inviting his colleagues and friends home for meals several times a week.

"I had many single colleagues and friends who appreciated having a home-cooked meal," said Michael good naturedly. "Even though I was the one who brought them home, Jacqueline was the one who touched them with the effort she took in her baking and cooking. A Korean girl took one spoonful of Jacqueline's *kimchi* soup and she cried, saying, 'This tastes like home!' By inviting them into our house, we were telling them that they were welcome into our family. We developed good friendships in Vietnam, not fostered in the office or the classroom, but at our dining table."

Top: Cupcakes highlighting Tea Talk's motto and a photo with Tra My (right, in spectacles), who was so impacted by Michael that she now works with women who have been trafficked. Bottom: Michael and Jacqueline have fostered many a close friendship over a home-cooked meal.

Despite noticing the curious connection between food and friendship, Michael only came up with the idea for Tea Talk when the family moved to the United States for two years.

"While doing my Masters in Social Work at Washington University, St Louis, I signed up for a class on social entrepreneurship," said Michael. "Business had always been taboo to me. Having a social worker's background meant that I associated business with cutthroat profit making. But I wanted to learn something about business, after all social enterprise is also part of social work."

The first day of class had been intimidating.

"Half the class were MBA grads who dressed smartly. The other half were social workers, wearing t-shirts and jeans.

"Worse still, the prof came in and he behaved like Donald Trump! He said, 'Okay all of you are going to come up with an idea that's going to revolutionise the world. And you have 30 seconds to pitch your idea… business people have very little time!'

"I was really stressed! I just wanted to learn how to read a profit and loss sheet and find out what it means to be a businessman. I didn't sign up for this!

"I went home and cried on my wife's shoulder. There didn't seem any way to avoid a failing grade. Then I remembered the professor saying, 'In the business world, if you're the only fool who wants to pursue an idea, nobody can stop you.' So I roped in three other classmates whom I guessed were in the same predicament as I was and we formed a group. My intention was to be one of their 'employees' but they turned around and said, 'Michael, you seem most passionate about your idea, let's go with it.' So we worked out our proposal for Tea Talk.

"At the end of the semester, everyone presented their business plans and my group won! Pseudo Donald Trump presented our team with US$200 as first prize, which we spent on a meal at a Vietnamese restaurant!"

With a post-graduate degree in social work under his belt, Michael returned to Vietnam with his family and Tea Talk CoRE (Centre for Counselling, Research and Empowerment of Community) was born.

The five-year-old social venture now has 10 full-time staff working on café operations and five concentrating on social work.

"Tea Talk is the café and CoRE is the software, the heart," said Michael. "They are Siamese twins that should never be separated. If Tea Talk goes totally profit making, we lose our social value. But if we concentrate only on CoRE, we are like any other charity. So we work at having the right balance and tension."

***

The social impact Tea Talk has is not limited to students.

"At our café, we do things a little differently from other businesses," said Michael with a smile. "We don't employ people with experience and the right skills and say, 'Come and work for us!' We employ people with no skills and say, 'Let's figure it out!'"

When Michael and his team hired their 38-year-old cook Hien, they were already aware of her background: the mother of two young children had once had a mental breakdown. Her husband was an alcoholic who was sometimes abusive and slightly disabled so he did not work. As a young girl she had been sexually abused and her parents had told her that she was spoilt goods and could only marry someone else who was spoilt or disabled. When she was offered the job of cook at Tea Talk, she became the family's sole breadwinner.

"We wanted to help her by providing her with a job," said Michael. "She was a pretty good cook — her specialty was Hainanese chicken rice which Jacqueline taught her how to make. Eventually she became chief cook, managing our small kitchen. Our customer base grew because her food was tasty and presentable."

But one day Hien did not show up for work. The next day she was absent again and this went on for a few days. Michael could not contact her.

"After about a week we decided we'd better hire another cook," Michael recalled. "We had been turning customers away and our earnings had gone down. Finally we heard that she had been hospitalised because of a psychotic episode."

Six weeks later she showed up at Tea Talk in a dazed, medicated state and said, "Michael, do I still have my job?"

The new cook turned to Michael and said, "Are you going to fire me because she's back?"

Michael had a dilemma on his hands.

"As a social worker I knew that Hien needed to be engaged or she would spiral downwards into depression," he said. "I wanted to do what was best for her so I said, 'Yes we have a job for you. Continue to come to work tomorrow.' We kept both her and the new cook!"

For nine months Hien could not perform even the simplest of tasks and the staff began to complain. Michael sat his staff down and asked them, "What if it were you? What if one day you were injured and had to be hospitalised and six weeks later you had no job? How would you feel?"

Silenced, they saw the wisdom of Michael's decision.

Michael took me along one day when he paid a visit to Hien's home which she shared with her in-laws. The small, windowless living room had stained plaster walls weeping with dampness and peeling paint. Clusters of exposed wire hung about here and there. We sat cross-legged on the floor with the family as Hien graciously laid out refreshments of fresh longans and tea.

A little later she showed me her cluttered bedroom — there was just enough space on the narrow floor to fit one mattress upon which she, her husband and their son slept, and two planks where her daughter slept.

"What is your hope for the future?" I asked her.

"Money, just money, so that I can raise my children," she replied, looking wistfully at the framed photos of her young children.

I could see why Michael had hired Hien to work at Tea Talk. It was not just a job to her, it was the means to feed her children, a source of self respect and a lifeline to sanity.

Linh, Tea Talk's baker, was also hired out of goodwill.

She had been recommended for the job by her older sister, Trang My, Tea Talk's director for CoRE.

Trang My and Linh's father had died when there were very young and their mother had recently died in a tragic motorbike accident.

Michael stepped in not just as a mentor and employer but as a father figure to Trang My and Linh as well.

***

Top: Michael takes a photo of me and a trainee staff with the jars of cookies that I bought to share with friends at home. Bottom left: Visiting the humble home of Tea Talk's cook, Hien (2nd from right). Bottom right: At Tea Talk, staff are hired not because they have experience but because they need a job — Jacqueline trains all the cooks to turn out a mean plate of Hainanese chicken rice.

The Let's Talk graduation party was in full swing when I arrived at the cafe.

Food was not the only highlight of the graduation party that evening.

When the young men and women had had their fill of cupcakes and coffee, they made their way upstairs to a good-sized room with stencilled walls and a happy mural of candy-coloured buildings.

Sitting cross-legged on the parquet floor in a wide circle, the lights were turned off. In the dark, the youths couldn't resist making ghostly *Ooooo-oooo* noises to general hilarity.

Everyone quietened down when Michael handed out small candles. This was going to be the last time that they were sharing their thoughts within the group, and they were both wistful and hopeful.

One by one, the boys and girls spoke, lighting their candles as they did.

"I learnt that when we share our feelings, other people are also moved to share their stories," said one girl.

"I went from not knowing what was empathy to learning what it takes to counsel others," said another.

"There is great satisfaction in helping someone find a solution to their problem," said a boy.

All of them ended to affirming applause from their classmates.

"Light penetrates. The candles are like the spreading of your influence, from one life to another," Michael said in Vietnamese. "As you are transformed, you can touch someone else. We all have one chance to live — make it count."

It was such a simple ceremony, but the authenticity with which the young people shared, their earnest intentions to help family and friends in their social sphere, the connection they had with each other after 10 weeks of vulnerability in this very room, made this a beautiful rite of passage.

***

I have often felt that I am a female version of Michael.

My family had also struggled to make ends meet. While Michael had escaped being given away at birth, I had been fostered out as a baby, only returning to my parents at about three or four years of age. My sense of abandonment turned out to be a blessing in disguise. Like him, I feel a connection to people who are hurting and have the desire to reach out to them.

It has been a year since we filmed Michael in Hanoi. But the message of his work still reverberates within me.

"At the heart of counseling is the redemptive quality of just talking and listening," Michael said. "We all have a story to tell but we don't all have a safe environment to do it or people who respect our story.

"As the youths talked it out in a place where people showed interest, listened and asked the right questions, they were able to find meaning in what they had gone through and value in the discovery that they are better people as a result of their struggles.

"I am only one person. But if I can equip another person, she can help 10 other people, and those 10 people can help 100 people."

***

> ❝ *At the heart of counseling is the redemptive quality of just talking and listening* ❞

The youthful Let's Talkers are equipped with basic counselling skills to help their troubled peers.

To me, Michael reinforces what all the other men and women in this book stand for: the power of one.

These Singaporeans possess a measure of courage, resilience and love for humankind that shows that our spirit is stronger and kinder than we often give ourselves credit for.

At the same time, there is a universal sense of humanity in all the stories.

The spanking new suitcase I started my journey with when I visited Ravi Rai nine years ago is now rather battered. But the more worn it became, the more I grew as a person.

Yes, this can be a tragic world. But it is also a world filled with possibilities and unlimited opportunities for each of us to help and to give and to serve.

This, I now know, is the purpose of my life!

> ❝ *Yes, this can be a tragic world. But it is also a world filled with possibilities and unlimited opportunities for each of us to help and to give and to serve.* ❞

Michael presenting me with a book entitled *Connecting*, about building true relationships.

YOU CAN HELP TOO

Whenever I share my stories of selfless people who are making a social impact, I am asked how to get in touch with the various organisations.

Not all those I have written about are contactable, but here is a list of some of the NGOs and social enterprises with which you can get in touch.

I encourage you to drop them an e-mail or touch base with them if you are interested in learning more, or would like to share your resources and time with these deserving causes.

INDIA
Children of Mother Earth (CoME)
http://www.comeinternational.org/

CHINA
Bethesda Frankel Estate Church (donations should indicate that they are specifically for the Fugong Mental Health programme)
http://www.bfec.org.sg

KENYA
Kenyan Riders
www.kenyanriders.com
or Facebook/kenyanriders

SHANGRI-LA
The Compass Café & Lodge
http://www.thecompass.asia/

MONGOLIA
Lamp of the Path
http://www.fpmtmongolia.org/lamp-of-the-path-ngo/

VIETNAM
Tea Talk CoRE
www.teatalkvietnam.blogspot.sg

acknowledgements

In my many travels I have made new friends, explored amazing places and walked in the footsteps of remarkable people. For that I am deeply thankful. But there were also times when I was exhausted, sick, and shed tears in my hotel room (even in Bhutan, the "happiest place on earth"!) simply because I missed my family and friends so much.

No matter how beautiful a destination I travel to, I find I always want to come home at the end of the day because this is where my family and closest friends are. Thank you for being my anchor and my assurance.

For seeing me through the two years it took to produce *Larger than Life*, I would also like to thank:

- Marshall Cavendish International Asia for breathing life into this book, in particular Associate Publisher Violet Phoon, Managing Editor Melvin Neo and Graphic Designer Adithi Khandadai Shankar.

- MediaCorp, especially my manager Mei Ho as well as my previous managers for your belief in me and for developing me into the artiste that I am today.

- Threesixzero Productions and August Pictures Pte Ltd for your generosity in allowing me to recount stories from *Find Me a Singaporean* and *The Places We Live In*.

- Elim Chew, who encouraged me to write this book. Without your persistence and belief in me, this book would still be living only in my imagination.

- Juleen Shaw, my co-author and editor, without whom this book would not have been possible. Producing *Larger than Life* together was so much more than putting words on paper. It was an emotional and enriching journey for the both of us. We did it!

- Ravi Rai, Tay Siang Hui, Tan Fang Fang, Cynthia Lim, Rizalito Sevilla, Nicholas Leong, Lesster Leow, Joseph Keh, Caroline Lalmalsawmi, Ramesh Meyyappan, Karen Lorimer, Zenn Tan, the landmine victims from Arrupe Centre, Michael, Jacqueline & Grace Ong, whose courage, resilience and love for humanity inspired this book and who made my job not work at all but a life-changing adventure.

- David Szeto, Duurengaral Togmid, Anubhav, Ah Chi and John Njoroge Muya, whose stories animate this book but who have since passed from this earth. I am thankful that our paths crossed in this lifetime. Although you are no longer with us, your spirit lives on in Larger than Life.

- Edwin Koo, Nasir Ishak, Uncle Goh Choon Song, Ansell Tan, Uncle Paul Leung, Ben Chong, and Sim Chi Yin/VII, who gamely dug out their pictures for *Larger than Life*. Your effort and time means a lot to me because, as we all know, a picture speaks a thousand words!

- My closest friends Shirley Tan, Anne Ng, Leon Jay Williams, Utt Panichkul, Donita Rose, Fanny Tan, Debra Chong, Bryan Lim, Annabel Soh, Faith Chen, Jacelyn Tay, Brian Wong, Dawn Lee, Celest Foo, Ivan Loh, Audrey Tan, Justin Koh and Alice Quek, who have encouraged me and stuck by me through every journey, despite my missing your birthdays, your weddings and your baby showers. Thank you for never giving up on me — knowing I was always on your mind and in your prayers meant the world to me and always will. No matter how tough it got, I knew that I would eventually come home to your love, encouragement and crazy *makan* sessions!

- My dearest family and relatives, especially my "Happy Cousins", for walking every step of my life with me. I am especially grateful to my mother, Gan Phlek Guat, who has held my hand through my darkest hours and who still greets me when I return from every trip by stroking my hair, patting my back, and asking, *"Xin ku ma? Wo de bao bei."* (Was it tough? My precious one.) Mummy, thank you for all your sacrifices and your unconditional love.

My papa, David Lee, a man of few words who is the joker of the family. I got my goofiness from you. Thank you for loving me.

My sister, Stephanie Lee, who is always the first to come to her *mei-mei's* rescue whenever I had a crisis. Thank you.

My brother, Max Lee, whom I call *zhu zi* (bamboo stick) and who calls me Big Mouth and sometimes Small Fly (is that smaller than Small Fry??). I hope I have done you proud.

- My late Godpa and my Godma, Michael and Lily Hooi, for standing by me and believing that I am made for greatness. Godpa bought me a Chinese dictionary when I was nine because he wanted me to be effectively bilingual. Through this and other fatherly advice, he moulded me into the person I am today, personally and professionally. Godpa, thank you for your great love and wisdom and for reminding me that the most important thing in life is relationships.

- To my friends who were involved in the initial stages of this book: Danny Yeo, Theresa Tan, James Lee, Irene Leong, Kelvin Kao, Daphne Ling, Ng Gek Song and Tan Ye Peng.

- To every single traveller I've met along the way, thank you for inspiring me with your unique perspective on life.

- Last, but not least, thank you to all those who have journeyed with me in big and small ways through my life. I wish I could name every single one of you, but please know that you are in my heart always.

about belinda lee

Attractive and bubbly, Belinda was the first Singaporean to become an MTV VJ in 1998 after winning over the producers in a regional talent scouting competition. During her five years at MTV, her show *MTV Kan Yi Kan* won the Best Magazine Entertainment Programme at the Asian Television Awards in 1999, sealing her reputation as a quick-witted and entertaining television host.

Her career at MediaCorp Studios began when she joined the company as a host. But she soon broadened her artistic skills by trying her hand at acting. She caught viewers' attention in her debut drama serial *Room In My Heart*, convincingly playing the dual roles of a teenage rebel and a goody-two-shoes turned KTV hostess. She also acted as a long-suffering wife of a former gangster in *Soup of Life* and a hypochondriac in Singapore's longest drama *Your Hand In Mine*.

Versatile and effectively bilingual, Belinda hosted Channel NewsAsia's current affairs programme *Show Me the Money* and won the Best Info-ed Host award at the 2009 Star Awards for the reality dance show *Come Dance with Me*. She also hosted popular info-tainment shows *RenovAID* and *The Places We Live In*.

The effervescent host especially touched viewers with her long-running travelogue *Find Me A Singaporean*, where she went in search of Singaporeans abroad, some of whom were bettering the lives of others. Currently in its fourth season, *Find Me a Singaporean* won Belinda the Best Info-ed Host award at the 2013 Star Awards.

Belinda is a household name among television viewers, having been consecutively voted MediaCorp's Top 10 Most Popular Female Artistes from 2013 – 2015.

Her current appointment as World Vision SG Ambassador reinforces her popularity as a socially conscious celebrity who is both relatable and caring.

If you would like connect with Belinda, you can do so on these platforms:
- E-mail: emailbelinda@belinda-lee.com
- Instagram: leebelinda
- Facebook: http://www.facebook.com/belindalee.page

about juleen shaw

Juleen Shaw has over 10 years of editorial experience as a reporter, feature writer, sub-editor and editor at Singapore Press Holdings and MediaCorp Publishing. Currently teaching at the Wee Kim Wee School of Communication & Information (Nanyang Technological University), she has edited a diverse range of non-fiction books including *Chef Wan's Sweet Treats, What Makes You Clever – The Puzzle of Intelligence, Baba Boyhood,* and *The Revised Study Bible.*